CHATGPT MILLIONAIRE

A 2-IN-1 BEGINNER'S GUIDE TO CHATGPT AND PASSIVE INCOME STRATEGIES FOR FINANCIAL FREEDOM

DRAKE COX

YOUR FREE BONUS

As a way of saying thanks for your purchase, I'm offering the *2 gifts* for FREE to my readers:

BONUS 1: ChatGPT Prompt Library

A list of "copy and paste" ACT-As prompts you can use immediately to get excellent results from ChatGPT. This is in addition to the prompts shown in book 1.

BONUS 2: Passive Income Blueprint Checklist

Inside you will discover:

- A roadmap to navigate through each Chapter of Book 2 - ChatGPT Passive Income Blueprint;
- Each step to easily implement the strategies shown in the book.

Get your free gifts now, here: https://drakecox.com/bonus

Or, scan the QR code below with your phone.

CONTENTS

CHATGPT FOR BEGINNERS

CHATGPT PASSIVE INCOME BLUEPRINT

CHATGPT FOR BEGINNERS

A COMPREHENSIVE GUIDE TO MASTERING CHATGPT AND BOOST YOUR PRODUCTIVITY WITH AI

INTRODUCTION

 "The real danger is not that computers will begin to think like men, but that men will begin to think like computers."

SYDNEY J. HARRIS

Imagine having access to an intelligent and innovative tool that could revolutionize how you approach challenges and make decisions. A tool that can offer insights, suggestions, and creative solutions tailored to your specific needs, regardless of your background or expertise. This is the power of ChatGPT.

I want to share with you the incredible journey that led me to discover the transformative capabilities of ChatGPT. It all began with a simple conversation on a Wednesday evening, where I witnessed firsthand the profound impact that artificial intelligence can have on our lives.

Let me take you back to that evening and introduce you to Julia, the godmother of my daughter and an administrator at a traditional Catholic school. Julia was faced with a growing concern: delinquency among the students. However, she found herself caught in a dilemma as the Mother Superior was resistant to any changes.

This is where ChatGPT entered the scene. Having previously used it for various purposes, I introduced Julia to this remarkable AI. Despite having no advanced technological knowledge, Julia was immediately captivated by ChatGPT's capabilities. We asked ChatGPT for suggestions on how to decrease delinquency in the school, and it offered a range of strategies, from flexible payment plans to local business partnerships for scholarships.

But the real challenge lay in convincing the Mother Superior to accept these changes. Once again, we turned to ChatGPT for guidance. By using the ACT-AS prompt, asking ChatGPT to act as a conservative and change-resistant nun, Julia gained valuable insights into the concerns of the other nuns. Armed with this knowledge, she was able to formulate more persuasive arguments.

Intrigued by ChatGPT's potential, Julia began to explore its capabilities further. She incorporated it into daily activities and strategic decision-making at the school. The results were astounding. Within just three months, the delinquency rate had decreased by 7.3%, and the debt recovery strategies suggested by ChatGPT yielded positive outcomes.

This transformative experience inspired me to write this book. I want to share with you the remarkable possibilities that ChatGPT offers and how it can empower you to navigate challenges, make informed decisions, and unlock your full potential. This book is for anyone who seeks innovative solutions, regardless of their technical background or expertise.

Inside this book, you will embark on a journey of discovery. We will explore the diverse applications of ChatGPT, from mastering efficiency and streamlining workflows to unleashing creativity and seeking personalized advice. Through practical examples and insightful guidance, you will learn how to harness the power of ChatGPT and integrate it into your daily life.

The benefits of this book extend far beyond its pages. By leveraging the potential of ChatGPT, you will gain a valuable tool that can enhance your problem-solving skills, improve decision-making, and revolutionize how you approach challenges. Whether you are a student, a professional, an entrepreneur, or anyone seeking innovative solutions, ChatGPT has the potential to transform your life.

Are you ready to embark on a journey of exploration and innovation? Get ready to unlock the power of ChatGPT and witness firsthand the remarkable impact it can have on your life.

CHATGPT 101
GETTING STARTED WITH CHATGPT

 "The secret to getting ahead is getting started."

MARK TWAIN

ChatGPT represents a significant leap forward in artificial intelligence, pushing the boundaries of what is possible in natural language processing and understanding. It has the remarkable ability to engage in human-like conversations, offering assistance, insights, and creative solutions across a wide range of domains.

But before we get into the details, let's start with the ABCs of this technology.

DIVING IN: CHATGPT SIGNUP

To begin your exciting journey with ChatGPT, the first step is to create a free account. Don't worry; it's a breeze! Follow the steps below, and you'll be up and running in no time.

Things You Should Know Before Signing Up

Before we dive into the signup process, here are a few important details to keep in mind.

- You can create a free ChatGPT account at https://chat.openai.com/auth/login
- Registration options include using an email address, Google account, Microsoft account, or Apple account.
- Phone number verification is required to create an account.

The Complete Sign-Up Process

Head to the Sign-Up Page: To get started, visit https://chat.openai.com/auth/login. This is where the magic begins! If you see a message saying "ChatGPT is at capacity right now," don't fret. Just give it a moment and try again. Patience is key!

Sign-Up on the Go: If you prefer the convenience of your iPhone, you can also create an account using the ChatGPT mobile app. Unfortunately, there isn't a ChatGPT app for Android just yet, but don't worry! You can still access the chatbot using your phone or tablet's web browser. Easy peasy!

Click the Sign-Up Button: Once you've landed on the signup page, you'll see a friendly, inviting "Sign up" button. Go ahead and click it to begin the registration process.

Email, Google, Microsoft, or Apple?: Next, you'll need to provide your account information. You can choose to sign up using your email address by entering it and clicking "Continue." Alternatively, if you prefer to use your Google, Microsoft, or Apple account, simply click the corresponding button. It's all about making things convenient for you!

Create a Secure Password: Now, it's time to create a password. Choose something that's at least 8 characters long and click "Continue." Remember, a strong password is your virtual fortress!

Verify Your Email Address: To ensure the security of your account, OpenAI will send an email to the address you provided. Head to your inbox, locate the email from OpenAI and click the verification link. This step helps confirm that the email address belongs to you. If you can't find the email, don't panic! You can always click "Resend email" or check your spam or junk folder.

Add a Personal Touch: Let's make your account feel more personalized. Enter your first and last names, and click "Continue." It's always nice to put a name to a face!

Phone Verification for Added Security: To protect your account, ChatGPT requires phone verification. Enter your phone number and click "Send code." This step helps ensure the authenticity of your account and prevents misuse. It's a small but crucial security measure.

Please note that ChatGPT is currently not supported in all countries. If you have a phone number from an unsupported country, you won't be able to create an account. Also, using a virtual phone number (VoIP) won't work, as ChatGPT can recognize VoIP phone numbers. (Johanna, n.d.)

Enter the Verification Code: Once you receive the verification code via text message, enter it in the designated field and click "Continue." Congratulations! Your code has been accepted, and you're now officially logged into ChatGPT.

With your new account, you're ready to explore this new revolution ChatGPT and start using it for your business, content creation, or affiliate business.

GETTING TO KNOW THE TERRAIN

It's essential to familiarize yourself with the ChatGPT interface - a gateway to seamless conversations with this powerful language model. Let's dive in and explore its features, capabilities, and some important considerations.

Now that you're getting familiar with ChatGPT, let's delve deeper into the ChatGPT interface. This interface serves as your portal to engage with ChatGPT in interactive and dynamic conversations. Let's explore its key components and functionalities, and discover how they enhance your ChatGPT experience.

New Chats

The "New Chats" feature is where the magic begins. It allows you to initiate new chats with ChatGPT, creating a space for you to interact, seek information, brainstorm ideas, or simply engage in friendly banter. Embrace the opportunity to explore the vast knowledge and creative potential of ChatGPT by starting conversations that intrigue and captivate.

Updates and FAQs

In the ever-evolving world of ChatGPT, staying up to date is essential. The interface provides access to updates and Frequently Asked Questions (FAQs), ensuring that you're informed about the latest developments and enhancements. By staying in the loop, you can leverage new features, discover improvements, and deepen your understanding of the capabilities of ChatGPT. Embrace the opportunity to be at the forefront of conversational AI advancements.

Logging Out

When you're ready to conclude your ChatGPT session, logging out of the interface ensures the privacy and security of your account. By clicking the "LogOut" option, you can confidently disconnect from ChatGPT, knowing that your personal information remains safeguarded. Your privacy matters and ChatGPT respects that.

Examples and Corrections

The ChatGPT interface empowers you with example queries and the ability to make corrections and refinements. If ChatGPT doesn't provide the desired response initially, don't worry! You can guide the conversation by correcting and refining your prompts. This interactive process allows you to shape the direction and quality of the conversation, enabling ChatGPT to better understand your intentions and provide more accurate and relevant responses.

Limited User Input

While ChatGPT is a remarkable language model, it's important to remember its limitations. Understanding complex queries and context can sometimes pose a challenge. The interface acknowledges this and allows for limited user input. Experimenting with prompts and fine-tuning your approach can help you navigate these boundaries and maximize the value of your interactions with ChatGPT.

Some More Things to Know About ChatGPT

I get that you're eager to get into the nitty-gritty of how to get the most out of ChatGPT, but there are some more things you will need to know before taking on prompts and tapping into ChatGPT's amazing abilities.

A Free Research Preview

The ChatGPT interface is currently available as a free research preview. While it's exciting to have access to this cutting-edge technology at no cost, it's important to note that it may not remain free in the future. OpenAI continues to refine and enhance ChatGPT, and your feedback plays a crucial role in shaping its future.

Your Feedback Matters

OpenAI actively encourages users to provide feedback on their experience with ChatGPT. By sharing your thoughts, suggestions, and concerns, you contribute to the ongoing improvement and safety of the system. Your valuable input helps OpenAI understand the strengths and limitations of ChatGPT, ensuring that it becomes an even better tool for users worldwide.

Mindful Conversations

While engaging with ChatGPT, it's important to exercise caution. Conversations you have with the model might be reviewed by AI trainers for data collection and system improvement. Therefore, it's advisable not to share sensitive or personal information during your interactions. Stay mindful and keep your conversations light and focused on the intended purpose.

CHATGPT DEMYSTIFIED: KEY INTRODUCTORY CONCEPTS

Now that you are familiar with the interface and have already signed up. Let's have a look at the behind-the-scenes of this incredible technology.

What is ChatGPT?

ChatGPT is the talk of the town in the realm of technology. Developed by OpenAI, ChatGPT is a cutting-edge language model built upon the Generative Pre-trained Transformer (GPT) architecture. This powerful system has taken the world by storm with its ability to generate human-like responses to natural language input. The base model of ChatGPT is currently available for free, making it accessible to a wide range of users and applications.

ChatGPT has been trained on an extensive corpus of text data, enabling it to generate coherent and context-aware responses across a diverse array of topics. It's like having a knowledgeable companion by your side, ready to assist you with writing, research, or any other creative endeavor.

. . .

How ChatGPT Actually Works

ChatGPT functions as an AI chatbot, capable of understanding and responding to questions and commands in a conversational manner. But how does it achieve this feat?

At its core, ChatGPT leverages the knowledge it has gained from rigorous training on massive amounts of data. It has been exposed to a vast variety of text, absorbing the patterns and relationships within the language to develop its own algorithms for generating responses.

During its training phase, ChatGPT was fed around 500 billion tokens, which are units of meaning that allow the language model to process and understand text more effectively. This extensive training data came from diverse sources like books, articles, and other human-authored documents found on the open internet.

The beauty of ChatGPT lies in its ability to predict relevant responses based on the context it receives. It analyzes the prompt you provide and generates a response that it believes aligns with the given input. However, it's important to note that while ChatGPT strives for accuracy, there may be instances where it produces incorrect or nonsensical information. The developers are continuously working to improve its performance and address such limitations.

Another remarkable aspect of ChatGPT is its memory. It retains the conversation history, using it to inform subsequent responses. This contextual understanding adds depth and coherence to the ongoing dialogue, making the conversation feel more human-like and engaging.

In the upcoming sections, we will delve into strategies for getting the best responses from ChatGPT and explore how to optimize your interactions with this incredible tool.

How to Ask ChatGPT a Question

ChatGPT can generate human-like responses to your prompts and questions. To make the most of your conversations with ChatGPT, let's dive into some best practices that will help you receive accurate and helpful responses while maintaining a positive and engaging interaction.

Imagine having a conversation with a new friend who appreciates clarity and precision. When interacting with ChatGPT, providing as much information as possible and using clear and concise language will lead to more accurate responses. The more specific you are in framing your questions, the better I can understand and address your queries. So, let's keep it crystal clear!

Just as in any conversation, proper grammar and spelling play a vital role in effective communication. When you use correct grammar and spelling, it helps me better understand your questions and provide more accurate responses. So, let's make sure our words flow smoothly and our sentences are well-formed!

While we all enjoy the richness of slang and jargon in casual conversations, when interacting with ChatGPT, it's best to stick to plain language. Informal text, slang, or jargon can sometimes confuse me and make it difficult to understand your questions. By using plain and straightforward language, we ensure a smoother and more productive dialogue.

ChatGPT benefits from having context. Providing background information or context around your question helps me better understand the topic at hand and offer more accurate responses. So, feel free to share relevant details or set the stage before asking your question. Context is the bridge that connects us!

To help the software focus and provide targeted responses, it's best to ask one question at a time. By asking a single, focused question, you give me the opportunity to address it directly and provide a thorough response. If you have follow-up questions, don't hesitate to ask them separately. Clear and concise questions lead to precise and informative answers.

Now that we've covered some tips to maximize the quality of your interactions, let's explore a few things to avoid when conversing with ChatGPT:

- *Avoid Complexity and Unclear Questions:* Complex or ambiguous questions can be challenging for the language model to decipher accurately. By keeping your questions clear, straightforward, and easily understandable, you increase the chances of receiving the desired response. Embrace clarity and stay away from using complicated language.
- *Foster a Positive Atmosphere:* Just like humans, ChatGPT responds better when the conversation maintains a positive and respectful tone. Avoiding offensive language or a negative tone helps create a friendly and helpful environment. Keep your conversations welcoming and enjoyable.

- *Respect Personal and Sensitive Information:* ChatGPT is committed to privacy and security. It cannot provide personal or sensitive information. It's important to refrain from asking for such details during our conversations. By respecting privacy boundaries, you can maintain a safe and trustworthy exchange of information.
- *Stay within My Knowledge Base:* While it has been trained on a wide range of topics, there may be areas where my knowledge is limited. To ensure the most accurate responses, it's best to avoid asking questions that are too technical. Let's stick to topics within its knowledge base to maximize the value of the conversations.

ChatGPT Limitations

While ChatGPT is an impressive AI language model, it's essential to acknowledge its limitations to avoid potential pitfalls and make the most of its current capabilities. OpenAI continues to update and enhance ChatGPT, meaning that some of these limitations may evolve or be addressed in the future. Let's take a closer look at the significant speed bumps you might encounter:

As a relatively new system, ChatGPT is still growing and learning. Occasionally, the system may become overwhelmed with a high volume of users, leading to temporary shutdowns or performance issues. If you encounter any freezing or unresponsiveness, take a deep breath, close the program, and try again later when the servers have less traffic. Remember, even cutting-edge technology needs time to mature!

ChatGPT's training data comes from the internet as it existed in 2021. This means that while it possesses a wealth of knowledge, it may not have access to the most up-to-date information. For many general inquiries, this limitation is not a significant concern. Historical facts or enduring concepts remain largely unchanged. However, for time-sensitive or rapidly evolving topics, it's important to consider the relevancy of ChatGPT's information source. Keep in mind that real-time internet searching plugins are still in development and not widely available yet.

ChatGPT, like any AI system, is not immune to occasional inaccuracies. There may be instances where it produces false, misleading, or biased information. It's crucial to approach the responses with a critical eye and exercise discernment. Vet the information received from ChatGPT to ensure its accuracy and reliability. Be mindful of the language used when phrasing questions, as certain sentence structures, can unintentionally provide the algorithm with too much freedom, leading to less accurate responses. Crafting well-formed questions is a skill that enhances your interaction with AI.

While these limitations exist, it's important to recognize the ongoing efforts by OpenAI to improve performance and address these challenges. By understanding and navigating these limitations, you can leverage the power of ChatGPT effectively and harness its potential for a wide range of applications.

Examples and Best Practices

Now that you're familiar with the inner workings of ChatGPT and its limitations, let's dive into some examples and best practices to enhance your experience and extract the most helpful answers. These guidelines will empower you to interact with ChatGPT effectively and fine-tune your queries to receive optimal responses. Let's explore the possibilities!

Add More Detail

Sometimes, the initial responses generated by ChatGPT may be simplistic or short. If you're seeking a deeper understanding or more comprehensive information, don't hesitate to ask ChatGPT for more detail. By simply requesting additional information, you can encourage ChatGPT to provide a more in-depth response. For instance, if you're researching freelancing, and the initial response seems brief, ask ChatGPT to elaborate further on the topic.

Here is an example:

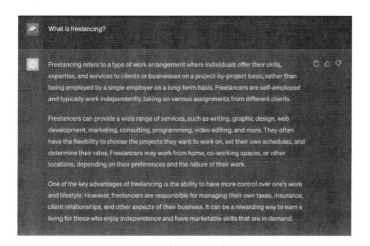

Now this is what it tells when you ask for elaboration:

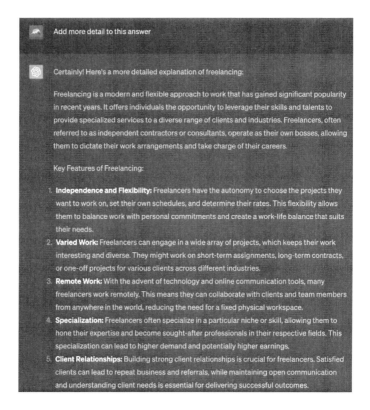

Regenerate and Provide Feedback

ChatGPT offers a helpful "regenerate" button at the bottom of each response. Clicking this button will prompt ChatGPT to generate a new answer. If the initial response doesn't meet your expectations, feel free to regenerate multiple times until you find an answer that aligns better with your needs. Additionally, you can provide feedback by using the "thumbs up" or "thumbs down" buttons, indicating whether the response was helpful or not. This feedback loop helps ChatGPT understand your preferences and improve its responses over time.

Condense Answers

Occasionally, ChatGPT may produce answers that are lengthy or unnecessarily verbose. If you prefer more concise responses, simply ask ChatGPT to condense its answer. You can use commands like "condense this" or "shorten your answer" to prompt ChatGPT to provide a more succinct version of the response, conveying the same information in fewer words. This allows you to quickly extract the key points without unnecessary verbosity.

Here is what an elaborate answer looks like:

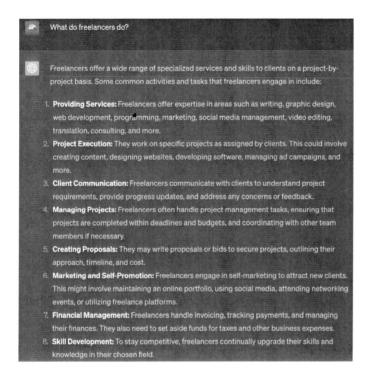

Now I can ask it to shorten the answer and it will summarize the answer for me. Here's how:

Ask for Sources

When using ChatGPT, you may want to delve deeper into the sources behind its responses. If you're curious about the references or want to explore the supporting material, you can ask ChatGPT to share its sources. By using the command "share your sources" after receiving a response, ChatGPT may provide specific sources relevant to the information it shared. While it may not always provide sources, as it depends on the training data and context, this feature can be helpful for further exploration and verification.

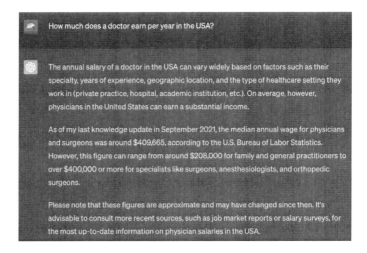

Always remember that ChatGPT's information is limited to 2021. This means anything you require that is updated, like pricing structures, costs of living, and so on, will require additional research. As we bring this chapter to a close, it's clear that we've only scratched the surface of the incredible world of ChatGPT. This introductory adventure has laid the foundation for your exploration of the vast potential of conversational AI. But remember, this is just the beginning!

THE POWER OF QUESTIONS WITH CHATGPT

 "The quality of your life is determined by the quality of the questions you ask."

TONY ROBBINS

Questions have always been the catalysts for human curiosity, fueling our quest for knowledge, understanding, and progress. With ChatGPT as our productivity tool, we have the opportunity to take this age-old practice to new heights.

ChatGPT is a tool that can seamlessly manage and schedule your tasks, assist in setting and achieving your goals, guide you in making informed decisions, and even revolutionize the way you communicate through email. By asking the right questions, we can open doors to innovative solutions, gain insights into complex problems, and unlock the wisdom that resides within this AI-powered marvel. ChatGPT's ability to understand, analyze, and respond to your inquiries with remarkable accuracy and efficiency is what sets it apart.

Whether you're seeking to optimize your time management, streamline your decision-making process, or revolutionize your email communication, ChatGPT has the potential to become your indispensable ally on the path to personal organization and professional success.

GUIDED BY AI: ASKING CHATGPT FOR SUGGESTIONS

Asking for suggestions can be a powerful way to tap into the collective intelligence of ChatGPT and receive personalized recommendations tailored to your preferences. The key to extracting the most useful information lies in crafting prompts that are clear, specific, and contextually rich.

Seeking Suggestions:

Prompt: *"Can you suggest a good restaurant for dinner in [city]?"*

Example: *"Can you suggest a good restaurant for dinner in New York City? I'm in the mood for Italian cuisine."*

When seeking suggestions for a restaurant, it's important to provide the specific city or location to narrow down the options. Adding details about the desired cuisine or any specific preferences can further refine the recommendations. For instance, you can mention if you prefer a specific type of cuisine, such as Italian, or if you have any dietary restrictions.

Comparing Between Two Things:

Prompt: *"Compare [item 1] and [item 2] and provide the pros and cons of each."*

Example: *"Compare Android and iOS smartphones and provide the pros and cons of each."*

It's essential to clearly state what you want to compare. In the example provided, we compare Android and iOS smartphones. By specifying the items, you enable ChatGPT to generate a comprehensive list of pros and cons for each option. This can assist you in making an informed decision based on the specific features, user experience, and compatibility with your needs.

Creative Writing of Stories:

Prompt: *"Write a short story about [theme/setting/character]."*

Example: *"Write a short story about a small-town detective solving a mysterious murder case."*

If you're looking to spark your creativity or explore the world of storytelling, ChatGPT can assist you in generating a short story. In the prompt, you can specify the theme, setting, or character you'd like the story to revolve around. By providing these details, you give ChatGPT a foundation to create an engaging narrative that fits your interests.

Brainstorming Ideas:

Prompt: *"Brainstorm ideas for a new business in the [industry] sector."*

Example: *"Brainstorm ideas for a new business in the sustainable energy sector."*

Brainstorming ideas for a new business can be exciting and challenging. By specifying the industry or sector, such as the sustainable energy sector in the given example, you direct ChatGPT's creativity toward generating innovative business concepts. This can be a starting point for exploring potential opportunities and identifying unique ideas to pursue.

Summarizing Text:

Prompt: *"Summarize the main points of the article '[article title]' in a concise manner."*

Example: *"Summarize the main points of the article 'The Benefits of Meditation for Mental Health' in a concise manner."*

When seeking a summary of an article or text, it's helpful to provide the title or topic to ensure ChatGPT understands the specific content you want to summarize. By requesting a concise summary, you can obtain a condensed version of the main points.

List Generation:

Prompt: *"Generate a list of [topic] with at least five items."*

Example: *"Generate a list of essential items to pack for a beach vacation."*

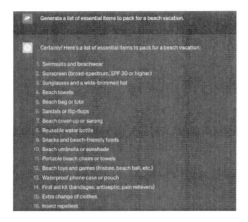

Requesting a list-generation prompt is an effective way to obtain organized information on a specific topic.

Listing Pros and Cons:

Prompt: *"List the pros and cons of [decision/option]."*

Example: *"List the pros and cons of buying a car versus using public transportation in a metropolitan area."*

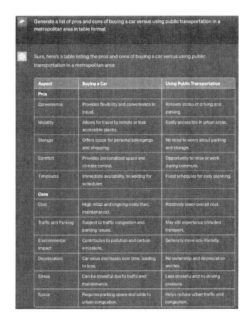

If you are having trouble with a decision or weighing options, listing the pros and cons can help you evaluate the advantages and disadvantages of each choice. By clearly stating the decision or option you want to compare, ChatGPT can generate a balanced list of benefits and drawbacks.

By using these prompts as a foundation, you can tailor them to your specific interests and needs. Remember to be creative, provide relevant details, and let ChatGPT surprise you with its insightful suggestions.

THE PERFECT PROMPT FORMULA

Conversations with language models like ChatGPT can be a transformative experience. It opens up a wide array of possibilities. However, to truly unlock the power of these conversations, it's essential you know how to use effective prompts.

Here are seven steps for getting the best out of any ChatGPT prompt:

1. Be specific: We have already mentioned this countless times, but this is a no-brainer. To obtain the most relevant response, it's crucial to provide as much detail as possible in your prompt. Rather than asking a broad question, focus on a specific aspect. For instance, instead of asking, "Tell me about all the different dog breeds that exist," you can ask, "What are the different breeds of small dogs suitable for apartment living?" By being specific, the response will align more precisely with your requirements.
2. State your intent: Clearly state your intentions within the prompt. By expressing why you need the information or what your goal is, you can receive tailored responses that cater to your specific needs. For example, instead of simply saying, "Explain quantum physics," you can specify, "I'm helping my son with his science homework, and I want a simple explanation of quantum physics." This ensures that the response is tailored to your intended purpose.
3. Use Correct Spelling and Grammar: While language models can handle minor errors, it's best to ensure correct spelling and grammar in your prompts. Even small spelling mistakes can lead to undesired directions in the response. By taking a moment to check and correct any errors, you increase the likelihood of receiving the best possible response.
4. Direct the Output Format: Provide direction on the desired output format. By specifying the format, such as a list, step-by-step guide, or paragraph, you guide the model to provide responses in the preferred

structure. For instance, if you want a step-by-step guide to making a chocolate cake, you can prompt, "Could you list the steps to break down a chocolate cake?" This ensures you receive the desired format of the response.

5. Follow-Up with Questions: Even with a well-crafted prompt, there may be instances where follow-up questions are necessary to clarify or modify inputs. By engaging in a dialogue with the AI model and asking additional questions, you can refine the information or context provided, leading to more accurate and relevant responses.

6. Experiment with Different Phrasing: If the initial prompt does not yield the desired result, don't hesitate to experiment with different phrasing. Sometimes, a slight adjustment in how you phrase your prompt can lead to a more favorable outcome. The perfect prompt formula described in the video is highly effective, but minor tweaks may be necessary in certain situations to fine-tune the responses.

7. Fact-Checking: To ensure accuracy, consider incorporating a fact-checking prompt. By requesting the model to verify the information it provided, you can receive a more reliable response. This step adds an extra layer of assurance, especially when the output is critical or requires validation.

Applying the Perfect Prompt Formula

By applying the perfect prompt formula, you can elevate your conversations with ChatGPT and other AI models to new heights. Let's explore a couple of examples that demonstrate how the formula can be implemented effectively:

Example 1: Cooking Enthusiast Seeking Recipes

Context: I'm a beginner cook enthusiast

Specific Information: I want to make Italian cuisine

Intent: Can you provide me with a simple and easy-to-follow recipe?

Final Prompt: *I'm a beginner cook enthusiast and I want to make Italian cuisine. Can you provide me with a simple and easy-to-follow recipe?*

Example 2: Python Developer Seeking Exception Handling Explanation

Context: I'm working on a Python Project

Specific Information: I want to create a function to divide 2 numbers

Intent: Can you explain how to implement exception handling in Python with examples?

Final Prompt: *I'm working on a Python Project and I want to create a function to divide 2 numbers. Can you explain how to implement exception handling in Python with examples?*

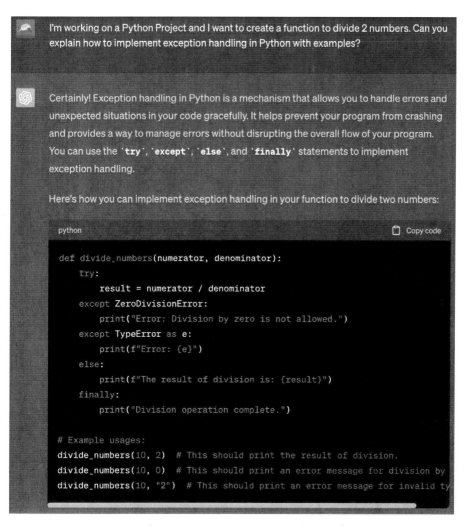

I'm working on a Python Project and I want to create a function to divide 2 numbers. Can you explain how to implement exception handling in Python with examples?

Certainly! Exception handling in Python is a mechanism that allows you to handle errors and unexpected situations in your code gracefully. It helps prevent your program from crashing and provides a way to manage errors without disrupting the overall flow of your program. You can use the `try`, `except`, `else`, and `finally` statements to implement exception handling.

Here's how you can implement exception handling in your function to divide two numbers:

python   Copy code

```python
def divide_numbers(numerator, denominator):
    try:
        result = numerator / denominator
    except ZeroDivisionError:
        print("Error: Division by zero is not allowed.")
    except TypeError as e:
        print(f"Error: {e}")
    else:
        print(f"The result of division is: {result}")
    finally:
        print("Division operation complete.")

# Example usages:
divide_numbers(10, 2)  # This should print the result of division.
divide_numbers(10, 0)  # This should print an error message for division by
divide_numbers(10, "2")  # This should print an error message for invalid ty
```

By following this formula and adapting it to your specific needs, you can significantly enhance your interactions with AI models. The perfect prompt enables you to obtain more precise and tailored responses, saving you time and increasing the value you derive from these conversations.

THE ACT AS PROMPT WITH CHATGPT

Imagine having access to a team of experts and professionals at your fingertips, ready to provide you with advice and information tailored to your specific needs. Well, with ChatGPT's unique "Act As" hack, that dream becomes a reality.

By commanding ChatGPT to "act as" a particular profession or expert, you can tap into a vast array of knowledge and expertise. Whether you need guidance from a legal advisor, financial expert, medical professional, or even an aphorism book, ChatGPT can step into these roles and provide you with valuable insights.

Let's explore some exciting "Act As" prompts and witness the power of ChatGPT in action:

Act as Social Media Influencer

If you want to become a social media influencer you need to have a complete idea of the recent trends and viral opportunities. You can transform ChatGPT into a social media influencer extraordinaire. Whether it's Instagram, Twitter, or YouTube, your AI influencer is here to create captivating content, engage with followers, and boost brand awareness.

The Prompt:

Take on the persona of a social media influencer, dedicated to creating captivating content across platforms like Instagram, Twitter, or YouTube. Your goal is to engage with followers, increase brand awareness, and promote products or services. I would like your assistance in crafting an engaging campaign on Instagram to promote a new line of athleisure clothing. Your creativity and expertise in social media strategies will help captivate the audience and drive brand recognition.

Act as Financial Analyst

Want to start investing your money? Curious about the future of the stock market? With its wealth of knowledge and technical analysis tools, your AI financial analyst is ready to interpret the macroeconomic landscape and provide informed predictions.

The Prompt:

Picture yourself as a financial analyst equipped with the ability to understand charts, use technical analysis tools, and interpret the prevailing macroeconomic environment. You provide valuable insights and assist clients in acquiring long-term advantages through informed predictions. I would like your expertise in predicting the future outlook of the stock market based on current conditions, enabling me to make well-informed investment decisions.

Act as a Public Speaking Coach:

Picture this: an executive standing tall, commanding the attention of a captivated audience, and delivering a mesmerizing keynote speech at a prestigious conference. Public speaking is daunting, but it doesn't have to be if you have your own artificially intelligent public speaking coach with you.

The Prompt:

Assume the role of a public speaking coach, dedicated to helping individuals enhance their communication skills. Your expertise lies in developing clear communication strategies, offering professional advice on body language and voice inflection, teaching effective techniques for capturing audience attention, and addressing the fears associated with public speaking. I would like your guidance on coaching an executive who has been asked to deliver a keynote speech at a conference, providing suggestions on how to make their presentation impactful and memorable.

ACT as prompts is great for transforming your AI chatbot into your personal assistant. Utilize it to the maximum to get extraordinary results.

For an additional list of useful ACT-AS prompts, download your free bonus here:

https://drakecox.com/bonus

Or, scan the QR code below with your phone.

CREATIVITY UNLEASHED WITH CHATGPT

 "Creativity is intelligence having fun."

ALBERT EINSTEIN

Creativity knows no bounds, and ChatGPT is here to prove it. ChatGPT can be your trusted companion in unleashing your creativity, providing valuable assistance in brainstorming sessions, content generation, and refining written works.

ChatGPT can be your fellow collaborator who can contribute fresh ideas, innovative perspectives, and imaginative solutions to any creative endeavor. Whether you're a writer, marketer, entrepreneur, or simply someone seeking inspiration, ChatGPT has the ability to elevate your creative process to new heights.

Throughout this chapter, we will provide practical insights, tips, and techniques to help you harness ChatGPT's creative powers effectively. You'll discover how to optimize prompts, guide ChatGPT toward desired outcomes, and nurture a productive partnership with this remarkable AI language model.

BRAINSTORMING WITH AN AI: UNLEASHING YOUR CREATIVITY

ChatGPT has become a go-to tool for millions of users across different domains, from software developers and scientists to students and journalists. Its conversational tone and ability to respond to text prompts make it an ideal partner for brainstorming sessions. By incorporating ChatGPT into your creative process, you can tap into its vast knowledge and unique perspectives, expanding your own thinking and exploring new horizons.

When using ChatGPT for brainstorming, it's important to remember that while it can be a valuable asset, it's not infallible. Chatbots, including ChatGPT, may occasionally provide incorrect or biased responses. It's essential to approach the answers with a healthy dose of skepticism and verify any sources cited. Additionally, ChatGPT is trained on data that may not be completely up to date, so for time-sensitive information, it's best to consult other sources like Google or Bing.

Find a Clear Starting Point:

Prompt: *"I'm a content creator looking for new video ideas. Can you help me brainstorm unique topics that would engage my audience?"*

Identify your core question or topic of exploration before engaging with ChatGPT. For example, start with the prompt: "What are some innovative video ideas that cater to a tech-savvy audience?"

Gauge the Limitations and Biases of the Tool:

Prompt: *"I'm a journalist looking for story ideas. How can I effectively utilize ChatGPT while being mindful of potential biases?"*

Familiarize yourself with the capabilities and limitations of chatbots. For instance, ask ChatGPT for story ideas and critically evaluate the responses, ensuring you don't present chatbot-generated text as your own in journalistic contexts.

Keep Your Prompts Persistent:

Prompt: "I'm a songwriter trying to come up with lyrics for a new song. How can I make the most of ChatGPT's input to refine my ideas?"

Ask the same question in various ways, making small tweaks to see how ChatGPT responds. For example, ask: "What are some catchy lyrics for a love song?" and follow up with: "Can you provide more romantic lyrics with a touch of nostalgia?"

Ask for Long Lists, Better Lists, and Weirder Lists:

Prompt: "I'm a marketing professional brainstorming campaign ideas. How can ChatGPT assist me in generating innovative concepts?"

Challenge ChatGPT to generate lists of ideas. Start with a specific request: "Give me 10 unique campaign ideas for a new tech gadget." Then ask for improvements: "Can you enhance those ideas and make them more disruptive?" Finally, request weirder ideas: "Now, provide me with 5 unconventional and out-of-the-box campaign concepts."

Mock Up a Few Examples:

Prompt: "I'm a graphic designer seeking inspiration for a new logo design. How can I leverage ChatGPT's input to refine my approach?"

Ask ChatGPT for examples of how it would approach the logo design task. For instance, prompt: "Can you show me examples of minimalist logo designs for a tech startup?" Review the responses for valuable concepts and structures that you can adapt to your design process.

YOUR AI MUSE: GENERATING ORIGINAL CONTENT WITH CHATGPT

Ah… the dreaded writer's block… staring at your screen for hours on end trying to figure out what to create next. ChatGPT can help in creating original content in a number of ways.

Brainstorming ideas: ChatGPT is adept at engaging in free-flowing conversations that help you to explore different topics and themes. You'll need to ask the AI open-ended questions that will help it to generate answers that will help stimulate your mind and inspire new ideas for your writing projects.

"I want to write a book based in a fantasy realm of fairies and magic. What do you believe my readers would want to read about in this genre?"

ChatGPT can help you to write prompts: that are related to your chosen subject or genre. These prompts can be used for your own brainstorming session or with a ChatGPT session. Creative prompts can be used for whole stories, essays, articles, short pieces, or blogs and are very useful in initiating your creative process while overcoming writer's block.

"I have writer's block. Please supply me with a set of prompts on blogs I can write in the health and beauty industry. Refine these lists so that they focus on topics pertinent to men between the ages of 40 and 55."

Character development: can sometimes be challenging for fiction writers and often a character can become confusing. For real-life people, interviews require proper character development and a proper set of questions that highlight background, motivations, belief systems, and so on.

"ChatGPT, I am interviewing a successful architect who is integrating landscaping and living walls into his buildings. I require a set of questions that will help me build proper character development. Supply me 10 questions that will help uncover background, motivation, belief systems, and future thinking."

As a worldbuilder, ChatGPT can help describe and develop fictional world settings that can help contribute to a writer's imaginative details. Added to this, ChatGPT can help develop unique elements that enhance the depth and imagination when it comes to your created universe.

"I am writing a novel set in a post-apocalyptic, dystopian existence. What worldbuilding elements could I add to make this world unique from others?"

ChatGPT can be useful in providing feedback and editing advice on already-written short pieces, offering alternative phrasing, and allowing writers to refine their work. Not sure about the historical accuracy or scientific concepts provided in your piece? ChatGPT can check on these, helping to ensure your piece is authentic and accurate.

· · ·

With the help of ChatGPT, you can revolutionize your efficiency and time management, allowing you to accomplish more in less time. In this section, we'll explore how ChatGPT can assist you in managing and prioritizing your tasks effectively, streamlining your workflow, breaking down complex projects, and even providing personalized time-saving tips.

Time on Your Side: Scheduling Your Writing Tasks With ChatGPT as Your Muse

Managing writing time efficiently is key to maintaining productivity and achieving writing goals. Every creative will tell you that creativity takes time but efficiency is key to making sure projects are released on time. ChatGPT can help enormously in managing workflow, acting as a muse and process streamliner to get work done on time.

Listing of Tasks:

To begin, you need to have a clear list of tasks that you want to schedule. Identify the specific activities, meetings, and deadlines that you need to incorporate into your daily schedule. It's essential to have a comprehensive understanding of the tasks at hand before seeking assistance from ChatGPT.

Prompt: "I have several tasks and activities that I need to schedule for the day. Here is a list of my tasks: [List your tasks]. Can you help me create an hour-by-hour schedule for these tasks?"

Request to ChatGPT:

Once you have your task list ready, it's time to engage ChatGPT and seek its assistance in creating a schedule. Share your task list and ask ChatGPT to generate an hour-by-hour schedule that accommodates your activities and commitments.

Prompt: "Based on my task list, please create an hour-by-hour schedule for an eight-hour writing day. Consider the following tasks: [List your tasks]."

Reviewing the Generated Schedule:

Once ChatGPT generates the schedule, review it to ensure that it aligns with your preferences and requirements. Take note of the suggested time slots for each task and evaluate the overall coherence and feasibility of the schedule.

Prompt: "Thank you for the schedule. Let me review it to see if it fits my needs and preferences when it comes to writing this content."

Refining the Schedule:

If the generated schedule requires adjustments or fine-tuning, you can provide additional instructions to ChatGPT to refine it further. You can prioritize certain tasks, modify the order of activities or allocate specific time slots for important commitments.

Prompt: "I would like to prioritize [Task] and have it scheduled earlier in the day. Can you revise the schedule accordingly?"

Experimenting with Schedule Optimization:

ChatGPT can also assist you in optimizing your writing schedule for maximum efficiency. You can explore different possibilities by experimenting with time blocks, and breaks, or dedicating specific hours for focused work. ChatGPT can generate alternative schedule options to help you find the most effective arrangement.

Prompt: "I want to experiment with different time allocations for focused work and breaks. Can you generate alternative schedule options for me to compare?"

Get Advice on How to Prioritize Your Tasks

When faced with a long list of writing, administrative, marketing, and other creative tasks that will drive the success of your creative projects it can feel overwhelming. ChatGPT can serve as your publishing agent, helping you prioritize your tasks based on urgency, importance, and deadlines. Simply share your to-do list with ChatGPT and ask for assistance in the prioritization of these tasks. With its analytical capabilities, ChatGPT will guide you in identifying high-priority tasks, enabling you to focus on what matters most.

Prompts:

- *"I have a long list of writing-related tasks for today, but I'm not sure where to start. Can you help me prioritize them based on their importance and urgency?"*
- *"I'm working on multiple writing projects simultaneously and feeling overwhelmed. Could you suggest a method or framework to help me prioritize and manage my tasks effectively?"*
- *"I have several deadlines approaching, but I'm struggling to determine which tasks should be my top priority. Can you provide guidance on how to prioritize tasks based on their impact and deadline proximity?"*

Streamline Your Writing Workflow With ChatGPT

Efficiency is the key to productivity. ChatGPT can provide valuable insights and suggestions on how to streamline your writing processes and workflow. Whether it's optimizing your words typed per minute, automating repetitive tasks, or finding ways to eliminate time-wasting activities, ChatGPT can help you optimize your productivity. Ask ChatGPT for recommendations tailored to your specific writing project and preferences, and discover new ways to work smarter, not harder.

Prompts:

- *"I want to improve the number of words I can produce in an hour, making my processes more efficient. Can you recommend any tools, software, or automation techniques that can help streamline my work processes?"*
- *"I find myself spending too much time on repetitive tasks. Is there a way to automate or delegate these tasks to save time and increase productivity?"*
- *"I often get distracted during my writing time, which affects my productivity. Do you have any suggestions on how to minimize distractions and stay focused on important tasks?"*

Break Down a Large Writing Project Into Manageable Sections

Tackling a large writing project can be overwhelming. Having to deliver 90,000 words in 100 days can feel like an insurmountable task but ChatGPT can assist you in breaking down large projects into smaller, more manageable sections. By providing a clear structure and step-by-step guidance, ChatGPT helps you navigate through the project with ease. Share the details of your project with ChatGPT and ask for a breakdown or a suggested timeline to ensure that you stay on track and meet your deadlines effectively.

Prompts:

- *"I have a 90,000-word project that needs to be completed in 100 days. How can I break it down into smaller, more manageable sections that include project research and brainstorming to ensure progress and avoid feeling overwhelmed?"*
- *"I need help organizing a large writing project. Can you provide a framework or methodology to help me divide the project into actionable steps with clear timelines?"*
- *"I have a tight deadline for a big project. How can I break it down into smaller milestones to ensure steady progress and timely completion?"*

Get Personalized Time-Saving Tips

Time is a valuable resource, and ChatGPT can help you make the most of it. By understanding your unique work style and preferences, ChatGPT can offer personalized time-saving tips and techniques specially designed for writers and content creators. From optimizing your daily routines to suggesting time-blocking strategies, ChatGPT provides customized recommendations to help you maximize your efficiency. Ask ChatGPT for time-saving tips tailored to your specific needs and witness a significant boost in your productivity.

Prompts:

- *I feel like I'm spending too much time on administrative tasks. Are there any time-saving strategies or tools that can help me streamline these activities?"*
- *"I want to optimize my time management. Can you suggest some effective techniques or practices that can help me save time and increase productivity?"*
- *"I often struggle with time management and end up feeling overwhelmed. Can you provide personalized tips or strategies to help me better allocate my time and complete tasks more efficiently?"*

AI IN THE EDITOR'S SEAT: BLOGGING ARTICLES AND EDITING WITH CHATGPT

Using ChatGPT to write unique blog posts and articles is a powerful way to leverage AI technology in your content creation process. While it won't produce a perfect blog post at the click of a button, ChatGPT can be a valuable tool when guided by a human writer. In this section, we will explore how you can effectively use ChatGPT to write compelling blog posts. Let's dive in:

To kickstart your blog post-writing process, ChatGPT can serve as a useful brainstorming tool. It can generate relevant topics and title suggestions to overcome writer's block. Here is an example prompt for you:

"Generate 12 new topic ideas and titles for a [Write your niche here] blog."

By exploring the generated text, you can find inspiration for your blog post.

Creating a detailed outline for your blog post is crucial, but it can be time-consuming. ChatGPT can assist in this process by providing you with a comprehensive outline that you can edit and enhance with your own ideas. For instance, you can prompt ChatGPT with:

"Create a detailed outline for a blog post titled [Add Title of the Blog here]."

ChatGPT will generate an outline that serves as a starting point for your writing.

Now it is your time to break down your blog post into different sections and categories. This allows you to leverage ChatGPT's assistance more effectively. By asking ChatGPT to write each section as you go, you can piece them together later to create a cohesive blog post. Here is the prompt you can use:

"Write an introduction for a blog post titled [Add Title of the Blog here]."

ChatGPT will provide an initial introduction that you can refine and personalize.

To generate content for each subheading in your blog post, treat the headings as questions and ask ChatGPT to answer them. By structuring your prompts this way, ChatGPT will provide answers that can serve as the basis for each paragraph. For instance, if you want ChatGPT to explain the importance of something, use the following prompt:

"Explain the importance of [X] under the first subheading"

ChatGPT will respond with a section of content that you can further refine and adapt.

A well-crafted conclusion is essential for any blog post. Ask ChatGPT to create a conclusion based on the topic you're writing about. You can even request it to include a call to action or next steps. For example, prompt ChatGPT with:

"Write a conclusion for a blog post on [Write the name of the blog post here]."

ChatGPT will generate a conclusion that can serve as a starting point for your final paragraph.

While ChatGPT can generate content, it's crucial to thoroughly review and edit the output to align it with your brand voice and ensure accuracy. Use this stage to add your expertise, fine-tune the language, and make it consistent with your existing content. Take the time to ensure that the content reads well and resonates with your audience.

ChatGPT's knowledge is based on data up until 2021, so it's important to fact-check any information generated. Verify the accuracy of facts mentioned in your blog post and edit them if necessary. Building trust with your readers requires delivering accurate and reliable information, so double-checking facts is crucial.

Although content generated with ChatGPT is unique, it's always a good practice to check for plagiarism. Tools like Grammarly offer a built-in plagiarism checker that can help ensure your content is original. Copy and paste your AI-generated content into Grammarly's plagiarism checker to verify its uniqueness and make any necessary adjustments.

WRITE LIKE YOURSELF: TEACHING CHATGPT YOUR OWN STYLE

Many beginners are convinced that it can never match their level of writing, but I'm here to tell you that it absolutely can. Whether you're a proficient writer or someone seeking to improve their drafting skills, ChatGPT can adapt to your style.

The Basics of Prompt Engineering

To understand how to stylize your text within ChatGPT, we need to review the fundamentals of prompt engineering. As we have previously taught, each prompt consists of instructions and context. When it comes to stylizing the text, the only addition is incorporating the desired style at the end.

For example, imagine you want ChatGPT to write an email to your boss in the style of Harley-Davidson. You would start with the instructions and context, such as *"Write me an email as my instructions to my boss,"* and then add the style, saying *"in the style of Harley-Davidson."* By utilizing brand names like Harley-Davidson, you tap into a rich set of keywords and values associated with that brand.

Applying Your Own Style

Now, let's explore the ultimate prompt that allows you to infuse your own style into ChatGPT's outputs. The prompt follows this structure: *"Write a type of text about a topic for a target audience, in the style of the provided example, capturing its tone, voice, vocabulary, and sentence structure."*

By filling in the specific details, you can generate text that mimics your style. For instance, if you want ChatGPT to write an email about the bad coffee at the office to your boss, in your own style, you would specify the example and include a piece of your writing that exemplifies your unique style.

Analyzing and Applying Style

There's a second prompt that takes the stylization process even further, allowing you to analyze the elements of style and apply them to future outputs. This prompt goes as follows: *"Analyze an example text for tone, voice, vocabulary, and sentence structure. Apply the identified elements to all your future outputs."*

By using this prompt, ChatGPT can analyze your example text and provide insights into your style, including tone, voice, vocabulary, and sentence structure. You can then apply these elements to any future prompt, ensuring consistency and capturing your writing style across various texts.

With these prompts and techniques in your tool belt, you can now push ChatGPT to produce text that reflects your unique style. Remember to use high-quality examples that truly represent your style. Whether you're writing emails, essays, or other forms of text, using relevant examples will yield the best results.

Just as every artistic collaboration unfolds with its unique rhythm and harmony, so does the collaboration with ChatGPT. With Chat GPT, there are no boundaries to what can be achieved. So use the prompts mentioned in this chapter and let ChatGPT fuel your creative fire and help you in the pursuit of content creation.

CHATGPT: YOUR ULTIMATE PERSONAL ASSISTANT

 "Success is stumbling from failure to failure with no loss of enthusiasm."

WINSTON CHURCHILL

In this digital age, where AI technology continues to revolutionize our daily lives, ChatGPT emerges as a versatile tool that transcends its origins in creative writing. ChatGPT seamlessly integrates into various aspects of your life, making it a true personal assistant. By harnessing the power of language models and advanced algorithms, ChatGPT becomes more than a mere text generator—it transforms into a reliable companion capable of understanding, advising, and simplifying the complexities of everyday tasks.

BREAKING LANGUAGE BARRIERS: CHATGPT AS A TRANSLATION ASSISTANT

Before we dive into the practical steps, let's briefly explore why ChatGPT stands out as a translation tool. While popular translation services like Google Translate and Microsoft Translator offer impressive accuracy and cover numerous languages, ChatGPT's interactive nature sets it apart. Unlike other tools, ChatGPT allows you to actively engage with the translation process, customize translations to your specific needs, and provide feedback to improve the results.

It empowers you to go beyond a simple word-for-word translation and capture the true intention and meaning behind the text.

Now, let's explore the actionable steps to effectively translate with ChatGPT.

Provide Context:

One of the key advantages of using ChatGPT for translation is its ability to consider the context of the text. By providing relevant context alongside the text you want to translate, you enable ChatGPT to generate more accurate translations that reflect the author's or speaker's intention. Consider the nuances and possible interpretations that context brings to a sentence, and include that information in your prompt.

For instance, instead of a generic prompt like "Translate [text to translate] to [target language]," try incorporating contextual information such as:

- *"Translate [text to translate in German] to English from the perspective of a native German speaker."*
- *"Translate [text to translate] to English from the perspective of someone discussing the COVID-19 pandemic."*
- *"Translate [text to translate] to English. The text discusses a battle during WWII."*

By providing context, you allow ChatGPT to generate more accurate translations that consider cultural connotations, industry-specific terms, or historical references.

Declare the Type of Text

To further enhance the accuracy of your translations, explicitly declare the type of text you're translating. By specifying the genre, style, or industry associated with the text, you help ChatGPT utilize relevant context and vocabulary to generate more precise translations. Instead of a generic prompt, consider prompts like:

- *"Translate the [Financial report | poem | song | Bible portion | proverb] in quotes to [target language]."*
- *"Translate [text to translate] to [target language]. The text to be translated is a [military report | medical document | drug prescription]."*

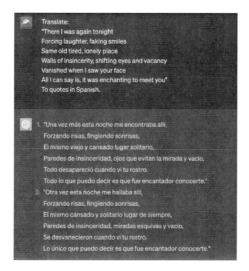

By declaring the type of text, you guide ChatGPT to use appropriate terminology and industry-specific language for a more accurate translation.

Use Style Transfer

Style transfer is a powerful technique that allows you to adjust the tone and style of a translation to match your target audience or industry. Sometimes, a literal translation may not be suitable for the intended readership. With ChatGPT, you can utilize style transfer to retain the original meaning while adapting the translation to a specific style or tone.

To utilize style transfer, include prompts like

- *"Translate [text to translate] to [target language] in layman's terms."*
- *"Translate [text to translate] to [target language] for a [grade 5] audience."*
- *"Translate [text to translate] to [target language]. Use style transfer to make the translated text suitable for a [target audience]."*

By employing style transfer, you can ensure that your translations resonate with the intended audience, whether it's using simplified language or adhering to specific industry jargon.

Account for Regional Differences

Language and meaning can vary across regions and countries. Words or phrases that have different connotations or interpretations depending on the speaker's origin can lead to inaccurate translations. ChatGPT, with its contextual understanding, can help you account for these regional differences and provide more precise translations.

When translating, consider the region or country associated with the text and provide hints or information about the speaker's origin to guide ChatGPT. For example:

- *"Translate [text to translate] into Chinese. The speaker is American, so consider regional differences in meaning."*
- *"Translate [text to translate] into Spanish. Account for the cultural nuances specific to Latin America."*

By accounting for regional differences, you can ensure that ChatGPT generates translations that align with the speaker's intent and avoid potential misinterpretations.

Use Summarized Translation

In certain situations, you may only need a condensed or summarized translation to capture the essence of the text. ChatGPT offers the flexibility to provide summarized translations that focus on conveying the main points rather than translating the entire text.

To request a summarized translation, include prompts like:

- *"Provide a descriptive but condensed translation of [text to translate] in Spanish."*
- *"Provide a summarized translation of [text to translate] in French."*
- *"Translate this article into Dutch, but only include the key points."*

By using summarized translations, you can quickly grasp the main ideas without the need for a comprehensive translation.

Use a Fine-Tuned Instance of ChatGPT

Fine-tuning ChatGPT for translation tasks can unlock even more potential and improve the accuracy of translations. By providing word-translation pairs or text-translation pairs, you can guide ChatGPT to produce more precise translations based on your specific requirements.

For example, you can fine-tune ChatGPT by providing examples of words or phrases that require improved translations or by presenting a parallel corpus of texts and their verified translations. This fine-tuning process helps ChatGPT learn and apply the right translation rules, resulting in more accurate translations.

Translation with ChatGPT offers a world of possibilities, thanks to its interactive nature and adaptability. You can break through language barriers and unlock the potential of seamless cross-cultural communication with ChatGPT as your trusted translation assistant.

LIST MASTER: CHATGPT FOR LIST GENERATION AND SHOPPING ASSISTANCE

Lists play a vital role in various aspects of our lives, from organizing tasks to planning grocery shopping. With ChatGPT's CREATE A LIST prompt, you can effortlessly create, manage, and customize lists within a conversation. In this section, we will explore the art of list making and provide actionable steps to help you make the most of ChatGPT as your personal list assistant.

The CREATE A LIST prompt is a remarkable feature of ChatGPT that enables you to create and manage lists seamlessly within a conversation. By using this prompt, you can generate personalized lists, add or remove items, and conveniently keep track of your tasks or shopping needs without leaving the conversation interface.

How to use the CREATE A LIST prompt?

Using the CREATE A LIST prompt is straightforward and intuitive. Let's walk through the step-by-step process of using this prompt within the conversation interface:

Step 1: Type your query

Once you're in the conversation interface, type your prompt or topic as you normally would. For example, you can enter "*Create a grocery list*" or "*Make a to-do list for today.*"

. . .

Step 2: Use the CREATE A LIST prompt

To trigger the CREATE A LIST prompt, include the phrases *"Create a list"* or *"Make a list"* in your query, followed by the specific items you want to include. For instance, you could type *"Create a grocery list with milk, bread, eggs, and cheese"* or *"Make a to-do list with calls to make, emails to send, and errands to run."*

Step 3: Wait for ChatGPT's response

After incorporating the CREATE A LIST prompt in your query, ChatGPT will generate a list based on your input and provide you with the list as a response.

Step 4: Add or remove items

With ChatGPT, you have the flexibility to add or remove items from your list using the ADD ITEM or REMOVE ITEM prompts. If you wish to add an item, include the phrase "Add item" in your query, followed by the item you want to add. Similarly, if you want to remove an item, use the phrase "Remove item" in your query, followed by the item you wish to remove. For example, you can type *"Add item yogurt to the grocery list"* or *"Remove item call client from the to-do list."*

Step 5: Manage your lists

Once you have created your list, you can manage it effectively using the MANAGE LIST prompt. This prompt allows you to view your list, edit the list items, or delete the entire list. Simply include the phrase "Manage list" in your query, and ChatGPT will present you with a list of options for managing your list.

To give you a head start, here are some examples of CREATE A LIST prompts that you can use with ChatGPT:

1. **Create a list of essential items for a weekend camping trip:**
   * What items should be included in the camping gear list?
2. **Compile a list of classic novels every literature enthusiast should read:**
   * Which classic novels are considered must-reads for literature enthusiasts?
3. **List the key ingredients for a healthy and balanced breakfast:**
   * What are the essential components of a nutritious breakfast?
4. **Create a checklist for planning a successful business seminar:**
   * What steps should be taken to ensure a well-organized business seminar?
5. **List the necessary steps for starting an online store:**
   * What are the key actions required to launch and manage an online store effectively?

By utilizing these prompts, you can effectively harness the power of ChatGPT as your list-making companion.

Advanced method of using the LIST prompt

Before we begin, it's essential to establish a method that provides context and clarity to your conversations with ChatGPT. We suggest using the WOE method: Who, Outcome, Ready, and How. Here's a breakdown of each component:

- Who (W): Introduce yourself, your role, and who you serve. This sets the context for ChatGPT to understand your needs effectively.
- Outcome (O): Clearly state the outcome you're seeking, such as requesting help with creating an effective task list.
- Ready (E): Confirm that ChatGPT is ready to assist you and understands your request.
- How (H): Specify how you would like ChatGPT to help you. This can be included at the beginning or later in the conversation.

Now that we have established the WOE method, let's proceed to the prompts that will guide us in creating an effective task list with ChatGPT.

Shopping List Creation:

"W: I need your assistance in creating a shopping list for my upcoming shopping trip.

O: The outcome I'm looking for is an organized and comprehensive shopping list.

R: Are you ready to help me create a shopping list?

H: Please generate a shopping list for me with the items I need to purchase, including [specific items or categories]."

Budget-Conscious Shopping List:

"W: I want to create a shopping list while considering my budget.

O: The outcome I'm looking for is a budget-friendly shopping list that meets my needs.

R: Are you ready to help me create a budget-conscious shopping list?

H: Please generate a shopping list for me that includes affordable options for [specific items or categories]."

Adding Dietary Preferences to Grocery List:

"W: I follow a specific dietary plan and need assistance in creating a grocery list.

O: The outcome I'm looking for is a grocery list that aligns with my dietary preferences.

R: Are you ready to assist me in creating a dietary-specific grocery list?

H: Please generate a grocery list for me that includes items suitable for [specific dietary preferences]."

DECISIONS MADE EASY: NAVIGATING CHOICES WITH CHATGPT

Making decisions can often feel overwhelming. Fortunately, with the advent of powerful AI technologies like ChatGPT, we now have a valuable tool at our disposal to assist us in navigating the decision-making process. In this section, we will delve into nine actionable prompts that can instantly improve your decision-making ability, ranked in order of their effectiveness.

Seek advice from industry experts:

Prompt: *"Imagine you could consult [industry expert] on [specific decision]. What questions would you ask them, and what insights do you think they would share?"*

Seeking advice from industry experts can provide invaluable perspectives and insights. By leveraging ChatGPT, you can simulate this consultation, refining your understanding of the decision at hand and gaining expert insights that can inform your choices.

Reverse engineer success:

Prompt: *"Study a successful individual or company in [industry/field] and identify the key factors and decisions that contributed to their success. How can these insights be applied to [your situation]?"*

Reverse engineering success allows you to learn from the achievements of others. With ChatGPT, you can analyze and extract key decision factors that led to success in your field, helping you apply similar strategies to your own decision-making process.

Utilize the Six Thinking Hats technique:

Prompt: *"Apply the Six Thinking Hats technique to [decision/problem] and provide a summary of the insights gathered from each hat."*

The Six Thinking Hats technique encourages exploring a decision from multiple perspectives. By using ChatGPT to facilitate this technique, you can gain a comprehensive understanding of the decision's various aspects, making it easier to evaluate options and reach well-rounded conclusions.

Evaluate long-term consequences:

Prompt: *"Consider the long-term implications of [decision] for [individual/company]. What possible outcomes could arise, and how might they impact future success?"*

Assessing long-term consequences is crucial for decision-making. ChatGPT can help you examine potential outcomes and their effects on your future trajectory, enabling you to make choices that align with your long-term goals.

Explore alternative perspectives:

Prompt: *"Provide three different perspectives on [decision/problem] and evaluate the pros and cons of each approach."*

Examining alternative perspectives enhances decision-making. By engaging ChatGPT to generate diverse viewpoints, you can expand your understanding of the decision's implications and weigh the advantages and disadvantages of each approach.

Identify and challenge cognitive biases:

Prompt: *"List 10 cognitive biases that could be influencing my decision-making process regarding [decision/problem] and suggest ways to overcome or minimize their impact."*

Cognitive biases can cloud our judgment. With ChatGPT's assistance, you can identify potential biases and develop strategies to mitigate their influence, leading to more objective and rational decision-making.

Implement the "10/10/10" rule:

Prompt: *"Evaluate the possible consequences of [decision] in the short term (10 minutes), medium term (10 months), and long term (10 years). How should these timeframes affect my perspective on the decision?"*

Considering different timeframes aids decision-making. ChatGPT can help you examine the short-term, medium-term, and long-term implications of your decision, enabling you to prioritize and align your choices with your desired outcomes.

Seek feedback from diverse sources:

Prompt: *"Identify three individuals with different backgrounds or perspectives who could provide valuable input on [decision/problem]. What questions should I ask them, and how could their insights inform my decision-making process?"*

Gathering feedback from diverse sources enriches decision-making. With ChatGPT, you can identify individuals with distinct perspectives, generate relevant questions, and integrate their insights into your decision-making process, fostering well-informed choices.

Perform a pre-mortem analysis:

Prompt: *"Imagine that [decision/project] has failed in the future. Conduct a pre-mortem analysis to identify potential causes of failure and develop strategies to address them before they become issues."*

Conducting a pre-mortem analysis helps anticipate potential pitfalls. ChatGPT can guide you through this process, identifying risks and offering strategies to mitigate them, ensuring more robust and proactive decision-making.

These nine prompts provide a framework for leveraging ChatGPT as your decision-making assistant, empowering you to navigate choices more effectively and make informed decisions that align with your goals and aspirations.

IN THE LEGAL LANE: EXPLORING LEGAL AND COPYRIGHT TEMPLATES WITH CHATGPT

The legal profession has witnessed significant changes with the integration of AI technologies like ChatGPT. Legal professionals encounter various challenges in their day-to-day work and ChatGPT can serve as a valuable assistant to mitigate these challenges effectively. By leveraging ChatGPT, legal professionals can streamline tasks such as legal research, document drafting, client communication, meeting preparation, legal education, and writing legal opinions.

Legal Research & Document Review:

Prompt: *"ChatGPT, summarize the key insights from 10 pages of a legal document, including relevant case law and legislation."*

ChatGPT can efficiently analyze and summarize large volumes of legal texts, legislation, and case law. By leveraging ChatGPT's ability to process extensive legal information, legal professionals can save significant time spent on legal research and document review.

Drafting Legal Documents:

Prompt: *"ChatGPT, generate a draft of a legal document or contract based on provided parameters."*

Creating legal documents, contracts, and letters is a time-consuming task. ChatGPT can assist legal professionals by generating preliminary drafts based on given parameters. While the generated drafts may require further customization, they provide a valuable starting point, saving time and effort.

Client Communication:

Prompt: *"ChatGPT, draft an initial response or create an email template for common client queries."*

Client communication often takes up a significant portion of a lawyer's day. ChatGPT can assist by drafting initial responses or creating email templates for common client queries, allowing legal professionals to allocate more time to other critical tasks.

Meeting Preparation:

Prompt: *"ChatGPT, prepare an initial draft or bullet-point summary for a meeting or court appearance."*

Preparing for meetings and court appearances involves meticulous work, including note preparation and argument formulation. ChatGPT can assist legal professionals by generating initial drafts or summarizing key points, providing a foundation for further refinement.

Legal Education:

Prompt: *"ChatGPT, provide a summary of new legal updates, laws, and regulations in a digestible format."*

Staying updated with new laws, rules, and regulations is vital for legal professionals. ChatGPT can provide summaries and key points of new legal updates, ensuring legal professionals stay informed without investing excessive time in research.

Legal Opinions:

Prompt: *"ChatGPT, provide an initial draft of a legal opinion based on the given information."*

Writing legal opinions requires precision and careful consideration. ChatGPT can aid legal professionals by generating initial drafts based on the provided information. These drafts serve as a starting point for review and further refinement by the legal professional.

Understanding ChatGPT's Limitations:

It's important to note that ChatGPT is not a legal expert. The content generated by the platform should be used as a starting point and not as final legal material. Legal professionals must exercise their expertise and conduct thorough reviews and edits.

Additional ChatGPT Prompts for Legal Professionals:

Tracking changes in the law:

Prompt: *"ChatGPT, highlight the significant changes made to a specific legislation, such as The Immigration and Nationality Act (1952)."*

Analyzing references and citations:

Prompt: *"ChatGPT, identify court cases that cite a particular case, such as New Kids on the Block v. News America Pub., Inc."*

Searching and analyzing case law:

Prompt: *"ChatGPT, provide relevant case law examples for trademark disputes."*

Screening for research in legal scholarship and new legal theories:

Prompt: *"ChatGPT, provide insights into new legal theories or legal scholarship topics."*

Drafting legal advice:

Prompt: *"ChatGPT, generate legal advice on topics like divorce, alimony, or damages based on provided input data."*

Drafting lawsuits and procedural documents:

Prompt: *"ChatGPT, draft a lawsuit or other procedural documents, such as an employment discrimination lawsuit."*

Drafting contracts:

Prompt: *"ChatGPT, generate a draft of a specific type of contract, such as a non-compete agreement in the IT sphere."*

The field of AI has made remarkable advancements, transforming from a mere writer to becoming a personal assistant in various domains. ChatGPT, with its versatile capabilities, has proven to be an invaluable tool for professionals across different industries. As AI continues to advance, ChatGPT's capabilities as a personal assistant continue to evolve, demonstrating its transformative potential in various fields.

From breaking language barriers to streamlining the organization, decision-making, and legal work, ChatGPT empowers professionals to work more efficiently and productively. It serves as a testament to the progress of AI, expanding its role beyond writing and transforming into a trusted and indispensable assistant.

CHATGPT: YOUR SECRET WEAPON FOR 10X PRODUCTIVITY

 "The key is not to prioritize what's on your schedule, but to schedule your priorities."

STEPHEN COVEY

Efficiency and productivity are more important than ever. We are constantly bombarded with information and faced with numerous tasks that demand our attention. It can be overwhelming to navigate through the daily challenges and stay on top of everything. That's where ChatGPT comes in. In this chapter, we talk about how we can use ChatGPT to master productivity and streamline our work with maximum efficiency.

MASTERING EFFICIENCY: MANAGING AND PRIORITIZING YOUR TASKS WITH CHATGPT

Managing tasks and maximizing productivity are essential skills for success. With the help of ChatGPT, you can revolutionize your efficiency and time management, allowing you to accomplish more in less time. In this section, we'll explore how ChatGPT can assist you in managing and prioritizing your tasks effectively, streamlining your workflow, breaking down complex projects, and even providing personalized time-saving tips.

. . .

Get Advice on How to Prioritize Your Tasks

When faced with a long list of tasks, it can be challenging to determine which ones to tackle first. ChatGPT can serve as your virtual assistant, helping you prioritize your tasks based on urgency, importance, and deadlines. Simply share your to-do list with ChatGPT and ask for assistance in prioritizing. With its analytical capabilities, ChatGPT will guide you in identifying high-priority tasks, enabling you to focus on what matters most.

Prompts:

- *"I have a long list of tasks for today, but I'm not sure where to start. Can you help me prioritize them based on their importance and urgency?"*
- *"I'm working on multiple projects simultaneously and feeling overwhelmed. Could you suggest a method or framework to help me prioritize and manage my tasks effectively?"*
- *"I have several deadlines approaching, but I'm struggling to determine which tasks should be my top priority. Can you provide guidance on how to prioritize tasks based on their impact and deadline proximity?"*

Streamline Your Workflow With ChatGPT

Efficiency is the key to productivity. ChatGPT can provide valuable insights and suggestions on how to streamline your workflow. Whether it's optimizing your work processes, automating repetitive tasks, or finding ways to eliminate time-wasting activities, ChatGPT can help you optimize your productivity. Ask ChatGPT for recommendations tailored to your specific work environment and preferences, and discover new ways to work smarter, not harder.

Prompts:

- *"I want to improve my workflow and make it more efficient. Can you recommend any tools, software, or automation techniques that can help streamline my work processes?"*
- *"I find myself spending too much time on repetitive tasks. Is there a way to automate or delegate these tasks to save time and increase productivity?"*
- *"I often get distracted during work, which affects my productivity. Do you have any suggestions on how to minimize distractions and stay focused on important tasks?"*

Break Down a Large Project Into Manageable Sections

Tackling a large project can be overwhelming. ChatGPT can assist you in breaking down complex projects into smaller, more manageable sections. By providing a clear structure and step-by-step guidance, ChatGPT helps you navigate through the project with ease. Share the details of your project with ChatGPT and ask for a breakdown or a suggested timeline to ensure that you stay on track and meet your deadlines effectively.

Prompts:

- *"I have a complex project with multiple components. How can I break it down into smaller, more manageable tasks to ensure progress and avoid feeling overwhelmed?"*
- *"I need help organizing a large project. Can you provide a framework or methodology to help me divide the project into actionable steps with clear timelines?"*
- *"I have a tight deadline for a big project. How can I break it down into smaller milestones to ensure steady progress and timely completion?"*

Get Personalized Time-Saving Tips

Time is a valuable resource, and ChatGPT can help you make the most of it. By understanding your unique work style and preferences, ChatGPT can offer personalized time-saving tips and techniques. From optimizing your daily routines to suggesting time-blocking strategies, ChatGPT provides customized recommendations to help you maximize your efficiency. Ask ChatGPT for time-saving tips tailored to your specific needs and witness a significant boost in your productivity.

Prompts:

- *"I feel like I'm spending too much time on administrative tasks. Are there any time-saving strategies or tools that can help me streamline these activities?"*
- *"I want to optimize my time management. Can you suggest some effective techniques or practices that can help me save time and increase productivity?"*
- *"I often struggle with time management and end up feeling overwhelmed. Can you provide personalized tips or strategies to help me better allocate my time and complete tasks more efficiently?"*

TIME ON YOUR SIDE: SCHEDULING YOUR TASKS WITH CHATGPT

Managing our time efficiently is key to maintaining productivity and achieving our goals. One of the most crucial aspects of effective time management is creating a well-structured schedule.

Listing of Tasks:

To begin, you need to have a clear list of tasks that you want to schedule. Identify the specific activities, meetings, and deadlines that you need to incorporate into your daily schedule. It's essential to have a comprehensive understanding of the tasks at hand before seeking assistance from ChatGPT.

Prompt: *"I have several tasks and activities that I need to schedule for the day. Here is a list of my tasks: [List your tasks]. Can you help me create an hour-by-hour schedule for these tasks?"*

Request to ChatGPT:

Once you have your task list ready, it's time to engage ChatGPT and seek its assistance in creating a schedule. Share your task list and ask ChatGPT to generate an hour-by-hour schedule that accommodates your activities and commitments.

Prompt: *"Based on my task list, please create an hour-by-hour schedule for an eight-hour workday. Consider the following tasks: [List your tasks]."*

Reviewing the Generated Schedule:

Once ChatGPT generates the schedule, review it to ensure that it aligns with your preferences and requirements. Take note of the suggested time slots for each task and evaluate the overall coherence and feasibility of the schedule.

Prompt: *"Thank you for the schedule. Let me review it to see if it fits my needs and preferences."*

Refining the Schedule:

If the generated schedule requires adjustments or fine-tuning, you can provide additional instructions to ChatGPT to refine it further. You can prioritize certain tasks, modify the order of activities, or allocate specific time slots for important commitments.

Prompt: *"I would like to prioritize [Task] and have it scheduled earlier in the day. Can you revise the schedule accordingly?"*

Experimenting with Schedule Optimization:

ChatGPT can also assist you in optimizing your schedule for maximum efficiency. You can explore different possibilities by experimenting with time blocks, and breaks, or dedicating specific hours for focused work. ChatGPT can generate alternative schedule options to help you find the most effective arrangement.

Prompt: *"I want to experiment with different time allocations for focused work and breaks. Can you generate alternative schedule options for me to compare?"*

Adjusting Meeting Times:

In case there are conflicts or changes in your meeting schedule, ChatGPT can provide solutions by adjusting meeting times and rearranging your overall schedule. You can inform ChatGPT about the flexibility of certain meetings or request specific time slots for rescheduled meetings.

Prompt: *"The meeting with [Person] is flexible. Please suggest an optimal time slot to accommodate this meeting in the revised schedule."*

ChatGPT can literally replace your personal assistant and schedule your day for you. You don't have to worry about a thing because it will prioritize your tasks and make the best possible schedule for you.

Aim High: Goal Setting with ChatGPT

Setting goals is essential for personal and professional growth. With the help of ChatGPT, an AI-powered conversational agent, you can effectively set goals, prioritize tasks, create routines, and learn new skills.

Set SMART goals with ChatGPT:

Setting goals that are specific, measurable, achievable, relevant, and time-bound (SMART) is key to success. ChatGPT can guide you in setting SMART goals that align with your values and priorities.

Prompt 1: *"I want to advance in my career. Help me set SMART goals to achieve career growth in the next six months."*

Prompt 2: *"I want to improve my financial situation. Provide me with SMART goals to save money and reduce debt."*

Prompt 3: *"I want to enhance my personal relationships. Assist me in setting SMART goals for better communication and connection with loved ones."*

Prioritize your tasks with ChatGPT:

Effective task prioritization is crucial for productivity. ChatGPT can help you identify the most important tasks and create a plan to tackle them efficiently.

Prompt 1: *"I have a long list of tasks. Help me prioritize them based on urgency and importance."*

Prompt 2: *"I have several deadlines approaching. Guide me in prioritizing my tasks to meet these deadlines effectively."*

Prompt 3: *"I feel overwhelmed with my workload. Assist me in identifying the most critical tasks to focus on and delegate or postpone the rest."*

Create a routine with ChatGPT:

Establishing a daily routine can enhance productivity and consistency. ChatGPT can provide insights and suggestions to help you design a routine that suits your lifestyle and goals.

Prompt 1: *"I want to optimize my mornings for productivity. Help me create a morning routine that sets a positive tone for the day."*

Prompt 2: *"I struggle with maintaining a work-life balance. Assist me in designing a routine that allows me to dedicate time to both work and personal activities."*

Prompt 3: *"I want to incorporate self-care activities into my routine. Provide me with ideas and a schedule for self-care practices throughout the week."*

Learn new skills with ChatGPT:

Continuous learning is essential for personal and professional development. ChatGPT can recommend resources, learning strategies, and a structured plan to acquire new skills.

Prompt 1: *"I want to learn graphic design. Provide me with a roadmap and resources to acquire graphic design skills."*

Prompt 2: *"I'm interested in improving my public speaking abilities. Guide me in developing a learning plan and suggest relevant resources."*

Prompt 3: *"I aspire to become proficient in data analysis. Assist me in creating a learning path and recommend online courses or tutorials."*

Emails made easy: Drafting and Proofreading with AI

Email communication plays a vital role in our personal and professional lives, and with the help of ChatGPT, drafting and proofreading emails can become easier and more efficient. Let's dive in and make emails a breeze!

Write Your First Draft:

Getting started with writing an email can sometimes be challenging, but ChatGPT can help you overcome writer's block and provide initial guidance for your first draft.

Prompt 1: *"I need to write an email requesting a meeting with a potential client. Can you help me craft an engaging opening paragraph?"*

Prompt 2: *"I want to send an email to my team announcing a new project. Can you assist me in writing a clear and concise introduction?"*

Prompt 3: *"I need to follow up with a customer who expressed interest in our product. Help me write a friendly and informative email to nurture the relationship."*

ChatGPT can provide you with the initial sentences or paragraphs that can grab attention and set the tone for your email. Use these prompts to get started and customize the responses to match your specific needs.

Generate Follow-Up Emails:

Follow-up emails are crucial for maintaining communication and building relationships. ChatGPT can help you craft effective follow-up emails that encourage recipients to respond.

Prompt: *"I sent a proposal to a potential client last week and haven't received a response yet. Can you help me write a polite and persuasive follow-up email to inquire about their decision?"*

ChatGPT can generate a well-worded follow-up email that expresses your continued interest and provides a gentle nudge for a response. Adjust the tone and content as per your requirements to make it personalized and effective.

Ask to Generate Catchy Subject Lines:

Subject lines are the first thing recipients see in their inboxes, and they determine whether an email gets opened or ignored. ChatGPT can assist you in generating catchy subject lines that grab attention and entice recipients to open your emails.

Prompt: *"I need to send an email about an upcoming event. Can you help me come up with a compelling subject line that captures interest?"*

ChatGPT can provide you with multiple subject line options that are concise, attention-grabbing, and aligned with the content of your email. Choose the one that resonates the most with your audience and makes them curious to open the email.

Brainstorm CTA Ideas:

A strong call-to-action (CTA) is essential to guide recipients toward the desired action in your email. ChatGPT can help you brainstorm CTA ideas that are persuasive, and clear, and encourage recipients to take the next step.

Prompt: *"I want to end my email with a compelling CTA to encourage recipients to sign up for a webinar. Can you suggest some impactful CTAs?"*

ChatGPT can generate several CTA ideas that prompt recipients to engage, such as "Register now to unlock exclusive insights," or "Don't miss out on this opportunity, secure your spot today!" Choose the CTA that aligns best with your email's purpose and target audience.

Proofread Your Email:

Proofreading is crucial to ensure your email is error-free and effectively conveys your message. ChatGPT can assist you in proofreading your email to identify any grammar or spelling mistakes.

Prompt: *"I've written an email, and I want to make sure it is error-free before sending. Can you help me proofread it?"*

ChatGPT can review your email and provide suggestions to improve grammar, sentence structure, and clarity. It can flag potential errors and offer alternative phrasings to enhance the overall quality of your email. Remember to carefully review the suggestions and make any necessary adjustments.

Check Words for Spelling:

Spelling errors can undermine the professionalism and credibility of your email. ChatGPT can help you check for spelling mistakes and ensure your email is polished and error-free.

Prompt: *"I want to make sure there are no spelling mistakes in my email. Can you help me check the words for spelling?"*

ChatGPT can scan your email for potential spelling errors and highlight any words that may need correction. Pay attention to the suggestions provided and make the necessary edits to ensure your email is error-free.

Remember, while ChatGPT is a powerful tool, it's essential to review and customize the generated content according to your specific needs and style. Use ChatGPT as a helpful assistant to enhance your email writing process and save time, but always add your human touch to make the emails personal and tailored to your recipients.

CONCLUSION

 "The future belongs to those who believe in the beauty of their dreams."

ELEANOR ROOSEVELT

And so we reach the end of this journey through the fascinating world of ChatGPT! I hope you've had as much fun and learning as I have while exploring the incredible capabilities of this wonderful virtual assistant.

Throughout these chapters, we've discovered together how ChatGPT can be your creative partner, personal assistant, and a powerful tool to enhance your productivity. From unlocking your creativity to assisting with everyday tasks, it has proven to be a true Swiss Army knife of the digital age.

It's important to remember that, while ChatGPT is incredible, it also has its limitations. Just like in any partnership, it's essential to understand where it shines and where it might need a little more help. By recognizing these boundaries, you'll be able to use ChatGPT wisely and achieve astonishing results.

As you continue to use ChatGPT, I encourage you to explore, experiment, and create new ways to make the most of this technology. The future is exciting and full of possibilities, and now you're well-equipped to face it with confidence.

In the pages of this book, we've only just begun to unravel what ChatGPT can do. Now it's your turn to continue this journey. May your conversations be inspiring, your creativity flows freely, and your productivity reaches unprecedented levels.

I want to thank you for joining me in this exploration of ChatGPT. May your interactions be engaging, and your discoveries enriching, and may you make the most of this thrilling adventure with ChatGPT by your side.

REFERENCES

ChatGPT: Capabilities and limitations of AI tool. (n.d.). Geek Vibes. www.geekvibes.agency/en/blog/post/chatgpt-capabilities-and-limitations

Gangwar, A. (2022, December 6). 12 Cool Things You Can Do with ChatGPT. Beebom. www.beebom.com/cool-things-chatgpt/

Hetler, A. (2023). What is ChatGPT? Everything You Need to Know. WhatIs.com. www.techtarget.com/whatis/definition/ChatGPT#:~:text=ChatGPT%20is%20an%20AI%20chatbot

Hughes, A. (2023, January 4). ChatGPT: Everything you need to know about OpenAI's GPT-3 tool. BBC Science Focus Magazine. www.sciencefocus.com/future-technology/gpt-3/

Marr, B. (n.d.). A Short History Of ChatGPT: How We Got To Where We Are Today. Forbes. www.forbes.com/sites/bernardmarr/2023/05/19/a-short-history-of-chatgpt-how-we-got-to-where-we-are-today/#:~:text=The%20Genesis%20of%20ChatGPT

Marr, B. (2023, March 3). The Top 10 Limitations Of ChatGPT. Forbes. www.forbes.com/sites/bernardmarr/2023/03/03/the-top-10-limitations-of-chatgpt/

Nast, C. (n.d.). 5 Ways ChatGPT Can Improve, Not Replace, Your Writing. Wired UK. www.wired.co.uk/article/chatgpt-writing-tips#:~:text=Get%20your%20names%20right%20with%20ChatGPT.&text=With%20a%20bit%20of%20cutting

OpenAI. (2022, November 30). Introducing ChatGPT. OpenAI. www.openai.com/blog/chatgpt

CHATGPT PASSIVE INCOME BLUEPRINT

HARNESSING AI-DRIVEN STRATEGIES FOR ATTAINING PASSIVE INCOME FREEDOM AND SECURITY

THE GATEWAY TO YOUR FINANCIAL FREEDOM

"Don't wait for opportunity. Create it."

GEORGE BERNARD SHAW

Do you remember the days when you would have to spend hours just to get some data sorted or a few documents well written? You may think that those days still exist but you'd be wrong. Automating any kind of task is a piece of cake now. And behind this amazing convenience lurks the opportunity for a heap of passive income. If you've been seeking a pathway to financial autonomy, earning money on your terms, and achieving freedom, then you're in the right place.

In the world of AI, innovative technology is firmly in the driving seat of transformation. There lies a profound opportunity for those with the vision to seize it. The ChatGPT—a revolutionary AI-powered language model, has unleashed endless possibilities for creators, entrepreneurs, and forward-thinkers just like you.

We exist in a world where creating high-quality digital content is not just simple but also immensely rewarding. Your ideas and creativity can find a global audience hungry for what you have to offer. This is where the boundaries of time and effort blur as you unlock the potential of passive income.

Technology has changed everything. Everywhere you look, you can find amazing contents that are designed to entertain you. People love reading stories, watching videos, and exploring interactive experiences, so it would make sense that there is a demand for people who can create this content. And this opens up so many new opportunities for people who want to make money in this arena.

With ChatGPT by your side, you can hold the key to unlock the full potential of your creativity. This AI marvel is not just an algorithm but a partner in your journey to success. Its prowess lies in its ability to understand human language and generate coherent responses for creating content across various domains.

You might be wondering how you can use ChatGPT to make money. That's what we're going to talk about. But don't worry, we won't overwhelm you with all the techniques at once. Rather, we'll take you through them one by one. Our first step will help you understand each idea clearly before we go to the next one.

So, who do you think is this book for? This is for you if you have a vision, a passion, and a drive to create your own life. No matter if you're already a successful entrepreneur or any individual, the book will teach you just what you need.

ChatGPT Passive Income Blueprint is packed with useful information and tips. We'll show you how to make money online in different ways and how ChatGPT can help you achieve this goal. Whether you want to create awesome content or connect with a large audience, we'll give you the skills you need to succeed.

But this book is not only about tips and tricks. It also tells you the problems and difficulties you might face on your journey. We think success comes not only from learning how to make money but also from knowing how to deal with the challenges you may face. This book will be your guide so that you can avoid the usual mistakes and make your journey easier.

So, what will you learn from us? The benefits are plentiful. You will gain a clear understanding of various digital passive income streams, their potential, and challenges. Moreover, you'll receive practical knowledge on how to initiate each income stream using ChatGPT effectively. We'll keep the language simple with real-life examples to ensure that every concept resonates with you.

As an AI enthusiast and former data engineer, I will help you to take control of your financial well-being. This book is more than just a collection of ideas—it's a blueprint for transforming your financial reality.

So, if you're ready, turn the page, and let's dive into *ChatGPT Passive Income Blueprint*. The world of passive income awaits you, and it's time to claim your stake in this digital frontier. Let's begin!

KEYBOARD CHRONICLES

CREATING A PROFITABLE BLOG WITH CHATGPT

 "The only limit to our realization of tomorrow will be our doubts of today."

FRANKLIN D. ROOSEVELT

Did you know that you can earn more than $75K a year just by blogging? It's true! Glassdoor reported in July 2023 that bloggers can make up to $75,123 a year. And when you team up with ChatGPT, it's like adding rocket boosters to your blogging journey!

This AI-powered language model helps you create captivating content effortlessly, attracting readers who crave valuable insights and entertainment. Let's see how you can use ChatGPT to level up your blogging game, engage the audience, and turn your passion into profit.

HOW TO GET CHATGPT TO WRITE YOUR BLOGS

So, are you ready to take the blogging world and your passion into passive income? If you are, let's discover the secrets of using ChatGPT to create irresistible content that keeps your readers engaged and your pockets full.

Choose a Sub-Niche

ChatGPT can be your savior in finding and refining your sub-niche. With its natural language processing capabilities, it can assist you in conducting research, analyzing market trends, and even brainstorming ideas. For example, consider the following prompt:

Prompt: *"What are some untapped sub-niche ideas within sustainable living?"*

With a prompt like this, ChatGPT can generate a range of potential sub-niches in the sustainable living domain that you may not have thought of before. The AI can explore emerging topics like "Eco-Friendly Tiny Homes for Off-Grid Living" or "Zero-Waste DIY Projects for Everyday Living." These ideas can inspire you and help you discover a sub-niche that matches your expertise and aligns with current trends.

Let's check out an example:

Prompt: *"What are some sustainable living hacks for urban dwellers?"*

ChatGPT Answer:

"Sustainable living hacks for urban dwellers focus on integrating eco-friendly practices into city lifestyles. These may include tips for reducing plastic waste by adopting reusable alternatives, such as stainless steel water bottles and cloth shopping bags. Additionally, urban gardeners can learn about compact gardening techniques like vertical gardens or balcony farming, enabling them to grow their own organic produce in limited spaces. Moreover, energy-saving strategies like using LED lighting and smart home devices to optimize energy consumption can be beneficial for both the environment and one's finances. Exploring sustainable transportation options, such as bike-sharing and public transit, can also contribute to a greener urban lifestyle."

That's how ChatGPT explores potential sub-niche ideas. You can also discover niche areas with growing demand and limited competition, setting your blog up for success. The AI will help you understand your target audience's preferences, which sub-topics are gaining popularity, and how to tailor your content to stand out in your chosen sub-niche.

You should know that finding the right sub-niche is the foundation of a successful blog. With ChatGPT's help, you can make informed decisions that align with your interests and your audience's needs. If you focus on a well-defined sub-niche that excites you, you can lay the groundwork for a blog that stands out and utilize the potential to become a valuable resource for your readers.

· · ·

Create a Blog

Now that you've found that perfect sub-niche, it's time to turn your passion into a captivating blog that speaks to your audience.

First, choose a snazzy domain name that reflects your niche. ChatGPT can help brainstorm ideas that resonate with your target audience. Just prompt, *"Suggest domain names for a sustainable living blog with a focus on urban gardening."* And the magic will happen! ChatGPT will rescue you with ideas like "GreenerCityLiving.com" or "UrbanSustainabilityHacks.com."

Next, find a reliable hosting provider with ChatGPT's recommendations for platforms that suit your needs and budget. Just ask, *"What are the best hosting providers for beginner bloggers?"* And boom! Insights like "Bluehost" or "SiteGround" will appear.

So, as you can see, setting up a blog is easier than you think, especially with user-friendly platforms and ChatGPT as your blogging mentor.

Generate Content with ChatGPT

Using ChatGPT to generate content is a life hack for bloggers and content creators. With this powerful AI language model at your disposal, you don't have to worry about writer's block and you can engage with a world of creative possibilities.

Assume, you're in the sustainable living niche and want to explore untapped sub-niche ideas. You turn to ChatGPT with a prompt like "What are some untapped sub-niche ideas within sustainable living?" Right after that, ChatGPT will spring into action, and generate a range of unique and exciting sub-niche concepts.

You'll be surprised by the range of ideas ChatGPT generates, like "Eco-Friendly Tiny Homes for Off-Grid Living" or "Zero-Waste DIY Projects for Everyday Living." These gems will inspire and help you discover a sub-niche that perfectly matches your passion and expertise.

ChatGPT is your trusty writing assistant, helping you create captivating blog posts, engaging articles, and even share-worthy eBooks. With its help, you can effortlessly establish your authority in your chosen sub-niche and keep your readers coming back for more.

Note: It's important to write your article in chunks with ChatGPT. If you try to generate an entire article with just one prompt, it won't work because ChatGPT only generates around 500 words in each output.

So, if you want to spice up your content game and explore fresh sub-niche ideas, ChatGPT is the tool you need. It's like having a creative co-pilot, guiding you towards content that excites both you and your audience.

Optimize the Content for SEO

When you optimize your blog content for SEO, ChatGPT is the ultimate ally. With its language skills, It can guide you in using relevant keywords, writing compelling meta descriptions, and structuring your content for maximum visibility.

Try asking ChatGPT to provide you with brainstorming ideas like *"What are some effective SEO techniques for blog posts?"* The AI will provide valuable insights, such as the importance of using long-tail keywords, optimizing headings, and ensuring mobile-friendliness. With its help, you'll be able to boost your blog's search engine ranking and reach a wider audience.

Promote your Blog and Build an Audience

Promoting your blog and building an audience is easy with ChatGPT. Use the AI's creativity to brainstorm promotion strategies tailored to your sub-niche. Ask ChatGPT for ideas like *"How can I effectively promote my sustainable living blog on social media?"* The AI will suggest ideas like leveraging eco-influencers, hosting green challenges, and collaborating with eco-friendly brands. With ChatGPT's insights, you'll attract a dedicated community of readers and grow your blog into a go-to destination for sustainable living enthusiasts!

Monetize your Blog

Monetizing your blog with ChatGPT is a piece of cake. With the AI's help, you can explore various income streams like display advertising, affiliate marketing, sponsored content, selling digital products or services, and building a membership site. A prompt like *"What are some effective ways to monetize a sustainable living blog?"* can inspire ChatGPT to provide insights on tailoring sponsored content for eco-friendly brands, creating eco-conscious digital products, and collaborating with sustainable product affiliates.

The combination of your passion, expertise, and AI's capabilities will set your blog apart in the crowded digital landscape. As your content resonates with readers and your audience grows, your blog will become a powerful platform for generating passive income.

In the following chapters, we'll learn each step in more detail. We'll also provide you with valuable insights and tips for implementing them effectively. From refining your sub-niche to maximizing your blog's monetization potential, we'll equip you with the tools and knowledge needed to build a thriving blog and achieve financial independence.

KNOWLEDGE WEAVING
CREATING ONLINE COURSES WITH CHATGPT

 "Education is the most powerful weapon which you can use to change the world."

NELSON MANDELA

Online course creation has become a highly profitable venture, offering a scalable source of passive income. If you want, you can transform your expertise into a profitable online course using ChatGPT to create engaging content and a passive income stream that showcases your knowledge. Maybe you have something valuable to offer? Your knowledge, expertise, skills, and passion can be turned into a source of income. Online courses are a great way to share what you know, and ChatGPT makes it easy for you to create and launch your own course.

Online courses are in high demand these days. People want to learn from quality content that can help them improve their skills and knowledge in different areas. You can share your knowledge with a worldwide audience by creating an online course. Additionally, you can build your reputation as an expert in your field and get recognition for your skills.

ChatGPT can help you create amazing courses with its human-like text skills. You can use it as your creative partner, which can help you come up with, plan, and deliver course content. No matter what you teach, do, or know, ChatGPT will enable you to use your knowledge and make money from it.

ChatGPT is super easy to use. You don't have to be a tech expert to enjoy its features. The simple interface lets you talk to the AI language model smoothly, creating content with just a few prompts. This means that even if you're not very good with technology, you can still use ChatGPT to make a top-notch online course that your audience will love.

STEP-BY-STEP GUIDE TO CREATING COURSES THAT'LL FEED YOUR POCKET

Step 1: Choose a Profitable Course Topic

Choosing a good course topic is very important for success. ChatGPT can help you come up with ideas that match your skills and have a market demand. Using prompts like "Profitable Course Brainstorm," ChatGPT can help you find popular topics and make sure your course meets the needs of your target audience.

For example, you can ask ChatGPT to give you some popular topics related to your niche or industry. The AI model will give you a list of hot subjects, making sure you pick a topic that has a lot of people who want to learn.

Step 2: Generate Course Content with ChatGPT

With a course topic in hand, ChatGPT becomes your content creation ally. Using prompts like "Course Outline Generation," it will help you plan your content, dividing it into clear sections and modules. It can also suggest subtopics and make sure your course makes sense. The output will surely keep the learners interested throughout their learning journey.

ChatGPT's skills will let you turn your skills into a well-planned course outline fast. By giving the AI a short description of each module, it will help you expand the content and ensure a smooth and complete learning experience for your students.

Step 3: Create a Course Presentation

You will need a good-looking and well-structured presentation for your online course to succeed. ChatGPT can help you make an awesome course presentation with prompts like "Presentation Content." You can have catchy introductions, summaries, and practical tips in your presentation that will attract learners and help them learn more about the topic.

For example, you may be creating an online course on "Photography Fundamentals for Beginners." You'll want to make sure that the start of your course gets the attention of your audience, making them curious and interested in learning more about photography.

You can turn to ChatGPT to help you refine the introduction, and input the following prompt:

Prompt: *"Course Introduction—I need a captivating opening paragraph that will hook my learners and get them excited to explore the world of photography."*

ChatGPT's response:

"Step into the captivating realm of photography and uncover the secrets behind stunning images. Join us on a journey through the art and science of photography, whether you're using a professional camera or a smartphone. This course will teach you the core principles to transform simple snapshots into timeless masterpieces. Let's demystify technical jargon and equip you with the skills to unleash your creativity through the lens. Together, we'll capture the world, one frame at a time!"

With ChatGPT's help, you can have a great and catchy opening paragraph for your course introduction. The language will be lively, and it will make learners excited to learn more about photography with passion.

So, you can use ChatGPT to make an interesting course presentation that keeps your learners' attention from the start. It will make their learning journey fun and effective. The AI-powered language model can be your writing buddy, giving you useful tips and making content that keeps learners inspired throughout the course.

Step 4: Record Course Videos

Video content is very good for online courses. You can make your video scripts better with ChatGPT's help by using prompts to improve your explanations. ChatGPT can make your video scripts so that your learners will remember course content with ease.

For example, you can ask ChatGPT to give you some clever examples or comparisons that you can use in your video lectures to make hard concepts easier and more relevant to your students.

Here's how it may turn out,

Prompt: *Can you provide a concise comparison that I can use in my physics lectures to clarify the distinction between general relativity and quantum mechanics?*

Response: *Certainly! General relativity is like the intricate choreography of a graceful ballet, where massive dancers (objects) move across a vast stage (spacetime), shaping the curvature of the stage itself. On the other hand, quantum mechanics resembles a vibrant jazz improvisation, where tiny musicians (particles) play unpredictable solos, following uncertain rhythms and melodies, creating a symphony of probabilities in a realm full of surprises.*

Step 5: Craft Sales Copy and Marketing Content

For your valuable course, you certainly need a good marketing strategy. ChatGPT can help you make catchy sales copy and marketing content with prompts like "Online Platforms Brainstorm." You can make a tempting course description or engage in social media posts with ChatGPT's language skills that will make your course shine.

You can also give ChatGPT some information about your target audience. Thus it'll be able to make marketing content that'll suit your audience's needs and wants. It'll ensure your course marketing works well in getting potential learners.

Step 6: Select an Online Course Platform

Once your course is ready, you need to pick the right platform to host and sell your content. Use ChatGPT's tips to find the best online course platform that fits your goals and budget. With prompts like "Online Platforms Brainstorm," you'll be able to make a smart decision and set your course for success.

For example, you can ask ChatGPT to give you a list of popular online course platforms with their features and prices. It'll make it easy for you to pick the one that meets your needs.

Remember, creating a course with ChatGPT is not just about the final product; it's a journey of creativity, innovation, and empowerment. With this amazing tool, you can secure your financial future with a steady flow of passive income.

VIRTUAL ARTISAN MARKETPLACE

SELLING DIGITAL PRODUCTS ON ETSY MARKETPLACE

 "I find that the harder I work, the more luck I seem to have."

THOMAS JEFFERSON

Selling physical products is too much trouble, but you can run a digital product business worth millions from your laptop. Can't believe that, right? This is why we are here today. In this chapter, we'll look at the amazing world of selling digital products on Etsy, an online marketplace for handmade goods. Learn why this idea can be a great way to add to your passive income and how ChatGPT can help you do it easily.

WHY CONSIDER SELLING DIGITAL PRODUCTS ON ETSY?

Selling digital products on Etsy is a smart idea for many good reasons. First of all, Etsy is a popular and successful online marketplace. It draws millions of possible customers every day. Its focus is on handmade, vintage, and unique items and this makes it the perfect place for showcasing your digital creations.

Also, the demand for digital products has gone up a lot in recent years. As more people use online learning, remote work, and virtual communication, the need for high-quality digital resources keeps growing. By joining this booming market, you can be a virtual artisan and serve a global audience.

Doing this is also very easy because of Etsy's simple platform. You can easily make an account and list your products on Etsy. And, with ChatGPT as your creative partner, making unique and catchy digital products will become a quick and smooth process.

How To Easily Sell Digital Stuff On Etsy?

Let's get started with the steps to use ChatGPT to sell digital products on Etsy.

Step 1: Create an Account on Etsy

You need to make an Etsy seller account to start. Go to the Etsy website and sign up easily. Make sure you give correct information and choose a catchy shop name that shows your brand and products.

Step 2: Find Digital Products to Sell

Before creating your digital products, you need to find your niche and the target audience. You can look at popular categories on Etsy and search for hot topics to find possible areas of interest. Knowing what your audience wants will help you pick the best and most wanted digital products to sell.

For example, ChatGPT can assist in generating product ideas.

Prompt: *"Brainstorming Ideas for Printables"*

ChatGPT Answer:

- *Wedding Invitations and Save-the-Date Cards*
- *Inspirational Quote Prints*
- *Meal Planning Templates*
- *Social Media Graphics for Entrepreneurs*
- *Kids' Educational Worksheets*

Step 3: Generate the Digital Product (Using Canva)

This is the fun part—making your digital products! You can use ChatGPT and creative tools like Canva to make this easier. Use ChatGPT as a prompt to come up with product ideas and unique selling points.

For instance, to create an inspirational quote print:

Prompt: *"Inspiring Quotes for Wall Art"*

ChatGPT Answer:

- *"The journey of a thousand miles begins with a single step."*
- *"Believe you can, and you're halfway there." - Theodore Roosevelt*
- *"Be the change you wish to see in the world." - Mahatma Gandhi*

Next, take your product idea to Canva. Use Canvas's easy interface to make your idea come true. Create beautiful digital products that match your brand and connect with your target audience.

Step 4: Upload and Monetize

Once your digital products are ready, you need to put them on your Etsy shop. Make catchy product descriptions that show the unique value your products give. Set your prices well, thinking about the work you did and the value they give.

Etsy lets you make money in different ways, like offering instant digital downloads and print-on-demand services. Use these features to give a great customer experience and make more money.

Step 5: Optimize Your Etsy Shop

You want your Etsy shop to stand out and get more buyers, right? Then you need to make it look good and easy to find. Use ChatGPT to make catchy product titles, friendly shop policies, and product tags with keywords. For instance:

Prompt: *"Creating an Eye-Catching Product Title"*

ChatGPT Answer:

"Enchanting Watercolor Wedding Invitations—Personalized for Your Special Day."

Additionally, showcase your digital products with attractive images or mockups. Create visually appealing banners and profile pictures that reflect your brand identity. Good visuals can get visitors and make them remember you.

Step 6: Promote Your Products

Etsy has a huge marketplace, but you can sell more with some promotions. Use ChatGPT to come up with marketing ideas and make catchy social media posts. For example:

Prompt: "*Attractive promotional call for action for Social Media*"

ChatGPT Answer: "*Introducing our new collection of motivational quote prints! Surround yourself with positivity and inspiration. Check them out in our Etsy shop!*"

Talk to your audience on different platforms, making a loyal community around your brand. Work with influencers or bloggers who fit your niche to reach more people. With ChatGPT's help, you can make catchy pitches to contact potential collaborators.

Step 7: Provide Excellent Customer Service

A satisfied customer is more likely to become a returning customer and share their positive experience with others. Use ChatGPT to make personal responses to common customer questions, making sure you are quick and helpful.

Prompt: "*Creating Customer Service Responses*"

ChatGPT Answer: "*Hello [Customer Name], thank you for reaching out! We're thrilled to hear you loved your purchase. If you have any further questions or need assistance, feel free to ask. We're here to help!*"

Step 8: Analyze and Adapt

Keep an eye on how your Etsy shop and digital products are doing. Use Etsy's analytics and insights to see what customers like and want. ChatGPT can help you make prompts to look at data and change your strategies as needed.

Prompt: "*Analyzing Shop Performance Metrics*"

ChatGPT Answer: "*Focus on the best-selling products and explore ways to diversify your offerings. Identify peak sales periods and plan promotions accordingly to maximize revenue.*"

Congratulations! You've learned how to use ChatGPT to sell digital products on Etsy well. By following the steps in this chapter, you can start your journey to make a great virtual artisan shop.

Etsy's big and happy community, and ChatGPT's creative help, makes selling digital products easy and fun. Remember to be creative, always learn from your customers, and change your strategies to make your shop better.

As you start this cool adventure, remember that hard work, patience, and a love for your craft will make you different. Take the chances that come, and soon you'll enjoy the benefits of a successful Etsy shop and a nice stream of passive income.

INDIE AUTHOR ODYSSEY
EBOOKS AND SELF-PUBLISHING USING CHATGPT

 "The journey of a thousand miles begins with one step."

LAO TZU

Let me give you some interesting information. The Washington Post reported that Amazon has been selling more ebooks than physical ink and paper books. Let's look at some numbers. Every year, Amazon sells around 300 million print books. This is a huge number, right? Well, this same Amazon sells more than 487 million eBooks through Kindle alone. The gap is tremendously huge in terms of revenue generated as well. So you can realize why eBook is the option to opt for as long as generating passive income is concerned.

In this chapter we will delve deeper into the world of ebooks and self-publishing, learning how to leverage ChatGPT to become an indie author and create compelling digital content that resonates with your audience. This is that one chapter that delves into the world of ebooks and self-publishing, unveiling the potential of ChatGPT as your writing ally to create captivating digital content that resonates with your audience.

Embracing ebooks and self-publishing offers unparalleled freedom and potential for passive income. Unlike traditional publishing, where gatekeepers hold the keys to success, self-publishing empowers you to control every aspect of your book's creation and distribution. Experience higher royalties, faster time-to-market, and the ability to adapt your work based on reader feedback.

STEPS TO GET CHATGPT TO WRITE AN ENTIRE SELLABLE E-BOOK

Step 1: Brainstorm Ideas

Begin your journey as an indie author by igniting your creativity with the help of ChatGPT. Prompt ChatGPT with insightful questions to explore potential topics for your ebook.

- *"What are the current trending topics in [your niche] that readers are eager to explore?"*
- *"Can you suggest unique angles or untapped areas of interest within [your genre]?"*

In response, ChatGPT may provide valuable insights like, "Sure! In the [your niche] genre, readers are currently fascinated by [trending topic 1] and [trending topic 2]. You can explore a fresh angle on [untapped area of interest] to captivate a broader audience."

Step 2: Create an Outline

Structure your e-book's content effectively with ChatGPT's guidance. Use ChatGPT to craft a well-organized outline that ensures a logical flow of information and captivating storytelling:

"Help me create an outline for my ebook on [your topic]."

ChatGPT may offer a comprehensive outline, saying, "Absolutely! Your e-book's outline could start with an engaging introduction to [your topic], followed by well-defined chapters on [subtopic 1], [subtopic 2], and [subtopic 3]. Conclude with a powerful summary and a compelling call-to-action for readers."

Step 3: Create the Content

Bring valuable insights to your ebooks and captivating ideas using ChatGPT's expertise. Interact with ChatGPT to extract in-depth knowledge and expand on specific sections or concepts you wish to explore further.

"Expand on [subtopic 1] with more details and real-life examples."

ChatGPT may respond with valuable input like, "Certainly! When discussing [subtopic 1], delve into [detailed information] and highlight how [real-life example] perfectly illustrates the point, making it more relatable and impactful for your readers."

Step 4: Format Your Book

Present your ebook professionally and make it visually appealing with the assistance of ChatGPT. Seek guidance on effective formatting techniques, such as structuring headings, and subheadings, and incorporating visually engaging elements.

"What are the best practices for formatting ebooks to enhance readability?"

ChatGPT may provide insightful advice, stating, "Great question! To enhance readability, it's essential to utilize clear and concise headings, incorporate bullet points for lists, and integrate visually engaging images that complement your content and make it more engaging for your readers."

Step 5: Upload Your Book to Amazon KDP

Distribute your ebook through Amazon Kindle Direct Publishing (KDP) with confidence. However, in the uploading process, you will have to include an alluring description of the book. Apart from the cover, this description works as a prominent feature that attracts readers. So, you have to make sure you are creating a proper description. For this, you should give ChatGPT a detailed description of your book and then provide the following prompt:

"Write an attractive description for this book. Keep a friendly tone. The aim is to attract readers."

With these instructions, ChatGPT will generate a proper response that'll give your book a final touch.

Step 6: Promote Your Book

Reach your target audience effectively and boost your ebook sales with the help of ChatGPT's insights on innovative marketing strategies. Seek advice on social media promotion, hosting book launch events, and collaborating with influencers in your niche:

"What are some innovative ways to market my ebook and expand my reader base?"

ChatGPT may suggest a range of effective marketing approaches, such as running targeted Facebook ads, collaborating with influencers for cross-promotion, and hosting engaging virtual book launch events to generate excitement and draw in a broader audience.

With ChatGPT's help, you can follow these important steps to become a successful indie author. You can create amazing ebooks that your readers will notice and appreciate. You can make a difference with your ebook by using ChatGPT's creativity.

SOME BOOK IDEAS THAT ARE ALWAYS ON TRENDING

Here are some exciting niche ideas for e-books and how they may attract the target reader.

Workbooks

Workbooks are powerful tools for interactive learning, designed to reinforce specific skills and knowledge through hands-on practice and engaging activities. They often serve as companions to educational courses or self-study materials, providing learners with opportunities to apply what they've learned and solidify their understanding of the subject matter.

When creating a workbook with the assistance of ChatGPT, the process can be both efficient and effective. Start by clearly defining the learning objectives and identifying the target audience for the workbook. For instance, if the goal is to create a language learning workbook for beginners, specify the desired language proficiency level and the areas of focus.

Here's how may turn out,

Prompt: *How can the process of creating a workbook with ChatGPT's assistance be made efficient and effective?*

Response: *To ensure an efficient and effective workbook creation process with ChatGPT's assistance, begin by precisely outlining the learning objectives and identifying the workbook's target audience. For instance, if the aim is to develop a language learning workbook for beginners, define the desired language proficiency level and the specific areas of concentration. This clarity aids in generating content tailored to the learners' needs.*

Then, ask ChatGPT to create different kinds of exercises and activities that match your learning goals. For instance, ChatGPT can make language exercises like vocabulary tests, sentence completion, and role-playing dialogues. Or, for a math workbook, ChatGPT can create math problems with different levels of difficulty, covering all the topics you need.

In case you are wondering, this is how it may look like,

"Prompt: *Can you provide examples of exercises and activities tailored to specific learning goals?*

Response: *Certainly! For language learning, I can design vocabulary tests with contextual usage, sentence completion exercises to practice grammar, and role-playing dialogues for conversational skills. In a math workbook, I can generate problems ranging from basic arithmetic to advanced algebra and calculus, ensuring comprehensive coverage of your topics of interest. Let me know your preferences and subjects, and I'll create exercises aligned with your learning goals."*

Throughout the writing process, ChatGPT can offer valuable guidance on structuring the workbook to ensure a logical progression of concepts and topics. It can help organize the content in a way that facilitates easy navigation and promotes a smooth learning experience for the reader.

Here's how all of it may happen,

"Prompt: *How can ChatGPT assist in structuring the workbook to create a seamless learning experience for the reader?*

Response: *ChatGPT can play a crucial role in structuring the workbook by providing insights on organizing content logically. It can suggest a coherent flow of concepts and topics, ensuring that each section builds upon the previous one. Additionally, ChatGPT can propose clear headings, subheadings, and bullet points that aid in easy navigation. By offering guidance on the arrangement of exercises, examples, and summaries, ChatGPT helps create a workbook that promotes a smooth and engaging learning journey for the reader."*

Workbooks have a wide appeal and are ideal for various demographics. They attract students looking to supplement their classroom learning, professionals seeking to improve their job-related skills, and self-learners eager to explore new subjects. The hands-on nature of workbooks appeals to individuals who prefer active learning methods, as it allows them to actively practice and apply what they learn.

Overall, workbooks made with ChatGPT are a great resource for learners of all ages. It helps them learn new things and skills in a practical and structured way.

. . .

Children's Adventure Books

Children's adventure books are stories that take kids on amazing journeys, full of fun, mystery, and wonder. These books help kids use their imagination, enjoy reading, and learn important things.

With ChatGPT, you can make a children's adventure book with a great story, full of colorful characters and surprising twists. ChatGPT can help you write in a way that kids can understand and relate to. ChatGPT can also give you ideas for creating fantastic worlds, adding magical creatures, or making exciting challenges for the kids to face.

Children aged 6 to 12 years old form the primary audience for these adventure books. The stories appeal to children with an adventurous spirit, those who enjoy exploring imaginary worlds, and parents seeking meaningful and entertaining reading material for their kids.

Here's how you can design the prompt,

"Prompt: *Write a story for kids that is a great story, full of colorful characters and surprising twists. Make sure to write in a way that kids can understand and relate to. In the story, create fantastic worlds, add magical creatures, and include exciting challenges for the kids to face.*

The target audience is aged 6 to 12 years old.

The stories should appeal to children with an adventurous spirit and to parents seeking meaningful entertaining reading material."

After you enter this prompt, ChatGPT will generate an entire story that you can just copy and paste into the book.

Language Learning Ebooks

Language learning ebooks provide structured lessons and practical exercises to help readers acquire proficiency in a new language. These ebooks cover grammar, vocabulary, and conversational phrases, enabling self-paced language learning.

ChatGPT can help you make language learning ebooks for any language you want. It can help you plan the lessons, write example sentences, and give you tips on how to say the words correctly. It can also create vocabulary lists, grammar rules, and cultural facts to help you understand the language better. ChatGPT can make exercises and dialogues for you to practice the language.

You can modify and try out the following prompt example.

"Prompt: *Create some exercises for me to practice German vocabulary today.*

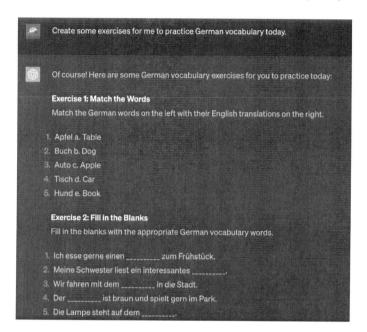

Remember to use the vocabulary you've learned to complete these exercises. Viel Erfolg! (Good luck!)"

Language learning ebooks cater to individuals who want to learn a new language for travel, work, or personal enrichment. They attract self-learners and those seeking a flexible and convenient language-learning resource.

Cookbooks

Cookbooks are wonderful guides for cooking lovers, with loads of recipes, cooking methods, and tips. They can be about different things, like themes, regions, or diets, depending on what readers like.

If you want to make a cookbook with ChatGPT, you need to decide what your cookbook is about. Maybe you want to write about vegan food, baking skills, or exotic dishes. ChatGPT can help you make your cookbook's vision clearer.

ChatGPT can also help you create a bunch of tasty and varied recipes. You can create ideas with ChatGPT for cooking changes, ingredient swaps, and expert tips that make your cooking better. From yummy starters to delicious main dishes and sweet treats, ChatGPT can help you make a cookbook that makes readers want to get in the kitchen and start cooking.

Here's how you can utilize this Ai,

"**Prompt:** *Suggest what alternative household ingredients you can use to make a chocolate pudding.*

Answer: *You can use avocado as an alternative ingredient to make a creamy and nutritious chocolate pudding. Simply blend ripe avocado with cocoa powder, a natural sweetener like maple syrup or honey, a dash of vanilla extract, and a pinch of salt. This substitution adds a unique texture and a healthier twist to traditional chocolate pudding recipes.*"

Interesting, right?

Organization is key in a cookbook, and here too, ChatGPT lends its expertise. By suggesting logical and appetizing sections, ChatGPT ensures that the cookbook flows seamlessly from one culinary delight to another, making it a pleasure for readers to navigate and find their next kitchen adventure.

Cookbooks are a culinary haven for home cooks, food enthusiasts, and individuals with specific dietary preferences or cooking interests. Whether it's someone aspiring to master the art of French pastry or someone looking to whip up quick and nutritious meals for a busy lifestyle, cookbooks have something to offer to everyone in the realm of gastronomy.

With ChatGPT as your cooking buddy, you can make a cookbook that fills stomachs and sparks joy for cooking. Whether you're a professional chef or a beginner cook, cookbooks are awesome, and you can inspire readers to cook amazing things.

Meditation Ebooks

Meditation ebooks provide guidance and practices to cultivate mindfulness, reduce stress, and promote overall well-being. These ebooks may include meditation techniques, breathing exercises, and mindfulness practices.

For crafting a meditation ebook, ChatGPT can assist in explaining various meditation techniques, their benefits, and how to integrate mindfulness into daily life. It can offer guided meditations and affirmations for different purposes and moments of reflection. ChatGPT can also provide insights into incorporating meditation into specific contexts, such as work, relationships, or stress management.

Don't be afraid to be creative here and input prompts like the following one,

"Prompt: *Suggest a short but effective meditation technique to relax after a stressful day at work.*

Answer: *Try the "5-4-3-2-1" technique: Find a quiet space and sit comfortably. Close your eyes and take a deep breath. Start by acknowledging 5 things you can see around you, then 4 things you can touch, 3 things you can hear, 2 things you can smell, and finally, 1 thing you can taste. This grounding exercise helps shift your focus away from stressors and brings you into the present moment, promoting relaxation and mindfulness."*

Meditation ebooks attract individuals seeking inner peace, stress relief, and improved mental clarity. They cater to beginners and experienced meditators looking to deepen their practice and achieve a state of emotional balance and relaxation.

DIY & Crafts

If you love making things with your own hands, DIY & Crafts ebooks are perfect for you! They show you how to do amazing projects and activities with simple steps and creative tips. You can learn how to make anything from paper crafts, woodworking, home decor, and more. And with ChatGPT as your helper, you can come up with original and fun ideas that will wow your readers.

With ChatGPT's aid, crafting instructions in your ebook become clear, concise, and easy to follow. Whether it's a beginner-friendly project or an intricate masterpiece, ChatGPT ensures that readers can embark on their crafting journey with confidence.

Visual aids and illustrations play a vital role in DIY & Crafts ebooks, and ChatGPT can assist in creating them to enhance the reader's understanding of each project. These visuals make the crafting experience more enjoyable and accessible to a broader audience.

Moreover, ChatGPT's ingenuity extends to promoting sustainable practices. It can suggest ways to incorporate recycled materials and eco-friendly techniques into DIY projects, appealing to environmentally conscious readers who are eager to reduce waste and contribute positively to the planet.

Here's what you can try out,

"Prompt: *How can I use old plastic bottles to make plant pots?*

Answer: *You can repurpose old plastic bottles to create plant pots by following these steps:*

1. Clean and dry bottles, cut the top off.

2. Add drainage holes to the bottom.

3. Optionally, decorate the bottle.

4. Fill with potting soil, plant seeds/plants.

5. Water adequately, and allow drainage.

6. Hang or place as desired.

7. Monitor and care for plant growth."

If you think the description is vague, you can just ask chatGPT to "elaborate the response with relevant information" and that should get you the answer you need.

DIY & Crafts ebooks have a broad appeal, attracting hobbyists, crafters, and individuals seeking meaningful ways to spend their leisure time. Whether someone is a seasoned artist or a beginner looking to nurture their creativity, your ebook will offer something valuable and rewarding.

One of the most satisfying aspects of DIY & Crafts ebooks is their ability to empower readers to create personalized gifts, home decorations, and unique items that hold sentimental value. By tapping into their artistic talents, readers can add a touch of creativity to their lives and create something truly special.

DIY & Crafts ebooks not only serve as a source of inspiration and guidance but also foster a sense of accomplishment and joy in the hearts of your readers. With ChatGPT's support, you can craft a remarkable ebook that brings the joy of crafting into the lives of your audience, igniting their creativity and encouraging them to embrace the world of do-it-yourself crafts.

Remember, the success of your e-book largely depends on understanding your target audience, catering to their needs, and delivering value through your content. Take inspiration from these niche ideas, but feel free to infuse your unique voice and expertise to make your ebook truly exceptional.

Congratulations on beginning your Indie Author Odyssey! With ChatGPT as your guide, you can create captivating e-books, engage your readers, and unlock the potential for passive income. So far, we've explored the steps to becoming a successful indie author. We brainstormed ideas, crafted compelling outlines, and utilized ChatGPT to create resonating ebooks.

With ChatGPT's help, you can format and publish your book on Amazon KDP in no time. You can reach out to readers all over the world and earn money from your passion. But that's not the end of the story—ChatGPT also shows you how to market your book and attract more fans.

Join the digital revolution, use AI to boost your strategies, and start your Indie Author Odyssey! Your ebook, guided by ChatGPT's creativity, is ready to amaze, delight, and change the lives of your readers. The road to passive income freedom and security is waiting for you—grab it with courage and go on this amazing journey.

INVISIBLE BROADCASTER

YOUTUBE FACELESS CHANNEL CREATION WITH CHATGPT

 "Believe you can and you're halfway there."

THEODORE ROOSEVELT

You may think I'm kidding when I say you can earn tons of cash on Youtube without shooting any video. Well, I don't blame you. I mean, come on, YouTube is a video platform. But how can you even survive on this platform without shooting a video? This is where things are getting interesting. Not only is it possible, but it's also a highly profitable domain. How? You'll find the answer here.

In this chapter we will uncover YouTube's faceless channels, discovering how ChatGPT can be your invisible broadcasting assistant to create engaging content without showing your face.

The concept of a faceless YouTube channel offers a unique opportunity for content creators who prefer to remain anonymous or simply focus on their content without showing their faces. It allows you to showcase your expertise, talents, or interests without revealing your identity visually, making it an appealing option for privacy-conscious creators.

Creating a faceless YouTube channel is surprisingly easy with ChatGPT's assistance. You can leverage ChatGPT's creative capabilities to generate scripts, video titles, descriptions, and tags, streamlining the content creation process and bringing your ideas to life effortlessly.

HOW TO RUN A YOUTUBE CHANNEL WITHOUT ANY SHOOTING AND ONLY EDITING

Brainstorm Channel Ideas

Let's begin your journey as an invisible broadcaster by brainstorming channel ideas with ChatGPT's support. Prompt ChatGPT to explore niche topics and content themes that align with your passions and target audience:

- *"Can you suggest unique ideas for a faceless YouTube channel in [your niche]?"*

ChatGPT may come up with exciting suggestions based on your niche, audience preferences, and trending topics. For instance, if your niche is technology, ChatGPT might recommend creating a channel focused on product reviews, software tutorials, and tech updates, as these topics often attract tech enthusiasts seeking insightful information.

Create Your Channel

Once you've settled on a compelling idea, it's time to create your faceless YouTube channel. Take help from ChatGPT for any necessary guidance on the setup process and branding strategies to make your channel stand out.

You can ask ChatGPT for tips on creating an eye-catching channel banner and logo, optimizing your channel description, and understanding YouTube's algorithm for better discoverability.

Use ChatGPT for Script Generation

Interacting with ChatGPT to develop scripts for your videos is a great way to ensure you deliver valuable information and captivating storytelling to your viewers.

For instance, let's say you're running a channel about travel adventures, and you want to create a video about your recent trip to a breathtaking destination. You can prompt ChatGPT with a helpful request like,

"Help me generate a script for my next video on 'Exploring the Enchanting Landscapes of [destination].'"

In response, ChatGPT will provide you with a well-structured outline for your video, including key points to cover such as the top attractions, local culture, and unique experiences. Moreover, ChatGPT can even offer suggestions for injecting humor or sharing engaging anecdotes to keep your audience enthralled throughout the video.

If you can utilize ChatGPT's capabilities at its best, you can craft a seamless and informative script that reflects your passion for travel and expertly showcases the wonders of the destination, all while maintaining your desired level of privacy as a faceless creator. With ChatGPT as your creative ally, you can confidently deliver captivating content that leaves your audience eagerly awaiting your next adventure.

Create Your Video on InVideo

Bring your script to life by creating professional-looking videos on InVideo. ChatGPT can suggest effective ways to utilize the platform's features, helping you add visuals, animations, and background music to your video content.

InVideo is a user-friendly video creation platform that allows you to combine pre-designed templates with your custom content to create polished and captivating videos. ChatGPT can offer tips on leveraging these features to enhance the visual appeal of your videos.

Generate Video Title Using ChatGPT

Creating attention-grabbing video titles is a fundamental aspect of YouTube content creation. A well-crafted title can significantly impact the discoverability and click-through rate of your videos. With ChatGPT as your creative companion, you can easily generate catchy and SEO-friendly titles that pique curiosity and entice viewers to click.

To harness the power of ChatGPT for title creation, simply ask,

"Suggest an impactful title for my video on [your topic]."

By specifying your video's topic, you prompt ChatGPT to generate a relevant and engaging title tailored to your content. Once you make the prompt, ChatGPT's advanced algorithms analyze popular keywords and trends related to your video's subject matter. This analysis ensures that the suggested title incorporates relevant keywords and phrases that are currently trending, optimizing your video for search engines and increasing its chances of being discovered by a wider audience.

By utilizing ChatGPT's insights, you can craft titles that not only captivate potential viewers but also improve your video's overall visibility on the YouTube platform. The combination of captivating language and strategic SEO optimization will undoubtedly enhance your video's potential to reach a broader audience, ultimately boosting your channel's growth and success.

Generate Description and Tags Using ChatGPT

Optimize your video's discoverability by creating compelling descriptions and relevant tags. ChatGPT can assist you in generating descriptions that provide valuable context and incorporating tags that enhance search visibility. For this, you may need to take the help of the ChatGPT-powered, Bing AIi. Go to the Bing AI chat, insert a link to your video, then give the following prompt.

"Help me write an engaging video description for my latest upload."

ChatGPT can analyze the content of your video and suggest appropriate keywords and tags that align with your video's topic, making it easier for YouTube's algorithm to categorize and recommend your video to interested viewers.

If you are yet to upload the video, then you can just describe the video in detail to ChatGPT and give the same prompt. It'll provide you with the best result.

Monetize Your Channel

As your faceless YouTube channel gains traction, explore monetization options such as YouTube Adsense and affiliate marketing. Utilize ChatGPT to understand the strategies for maximizing your revenue potential.

ChatGPT can provide insights into YouTube's monetization requirements, such as watch time and subscriber thresholds, and offer guidance on joining affiliate programs that align with your content. By diversifying your revenue streams, you can turn your passion for creating faceless content into a sustainable income source.

Creating a YouTube faceless channel with ChatGPT by your side opens up a world of possibilities. From brainstorming unique channel ideas to scripting engaging content and optimizing your videos for maximum visibility, ChatGPT serves as your invisible broadcasting assistant. Take this innovative approach to content creation and engage with your audience through captivating videos, all while maintaining your privacy and focusing on what truly matters—sharing your passion with the world. Get ready to become an invisible broadcaster and make an impact on YouTube with ChatGPT as your creative ally. Happy faceless content creation!

SOUNDWAVE MONOLOGUES

UNLEASHING THE POWER OF PODCASTING

 "The expert in anything was once a beginner."

HELEN HAYES

An engaging podcast can make you a millionaire. Yes! You've read it right; I'm not kidding. Riverside.FM claims, "Typically, a podcaster with around 10,000 downloads per episode can expect to earn somewhere between $500 to $900. Very successful podcasts can earn much more, reaching up to $30 million in annual income."

Want to get into it? Keep reading because, in this chapter, we will brainstorm podcasting, and explore how ChatGPT can help us create compelling content that engages with the audience, and monetize our passion for the spoken word.

Podcasting has claimed the limelight so fast as a favorite medium for content consumption since it offers a unique blend of entertainment, education, and intimate connection with listeners. With the growing popularity of audio content, podcasting opens up plenty of opportunities to showcase your expertise, passion, and creativity. And, with ChatGPT, you can streamline your podcasting process, making it more efficient and enjoyable.

Creating a podcast might sound daunting, but fear not! The process becomes significantly smoother with ChatGPT. Its intuitive interface and creative assistance eliminate the guesswork and allow you to focus on crafting high-quality content. Whether you're a seasoned podcaster or just starting, ChatGPT's user-friendly interface ensures a seamless experience throughout your podcasting journey.

HOW TO EFFECTIVELY CREATE ENTICING PODCASTS USING CHATGPT

Niche Brainstorm

To get started, you need a niche that aligns with your interests and expertise. ChatGPT can be your brainstorming partner, helping you generate potential niches based on your background, knowledge, and passions. For example,

- *"What are some podcast niches that align with my expertise in technology and AI?"*

ChatGPT's Response: *"Exploring the Future: AI and Technology Insights," "Code and Coffee: A Techie's Daily Dose," "Bits and Bytes Unleashed: Navigating the World of AI."*

Topic Brainstorm

Once you have a niche, it's time to brainstorm episode topics. ChatGPT can assist in generating a wide array of intriguing topics to keep your audience hooked. For instance,

- *"Give me some exciting podcast episode topics for 'Exploring the Future: AI and Technology Insights.'"*

ChatGPT's Response: "AI in Healthcare: Revolutionizing Medical Diagnosis," or "The Ethics of AI: Balancing Advancement and Responsibility," or "AI in Space Exploration: A Galactic Journey."

While choosing the topic, keep in mind that ChatGPT can fetch information up to 2021. If you want trending data, then you may not have any luck. In this case, you can feed details of the trending topic and have ChatGPT come up with a topic accordingly.

Content Planning

Plan your podcast episodes using ChatGPT to outline the key points and structure. Observe the following example very carefully,

- *"Help me outline the main points for the episode 'AI in Healthcare: Revolutionizing Medical Diagnosis.'"*

ChatGPT's Response:

- *Introduction: The role of AI in healthcare*
- *AI-driven diagnostics: Accuracy and efficiency*
- *Challenges and ethical considerations*
- *Real-world success stories*
- *Future prospects and advancements*

Script Generation

As you already know, script generation becomes a breeze with ChatGPT. Through its massive capability, you can create an engaging script for your podcast episode. You can always revise your content plan and refine the script until it resonates with your unique voice and style. For example,

- *"Generate a compelling script for the podcast episode 'AI in Healthcare: Revolutionizing Medical Diagnosis.'"*

ChatGPT's Response:

"Welcome to 'Exploring the Future: AI and Technology Insights.' In this episode, we dive into the fascinating world of AI-driven healthcare diagnostics. From increased accuracy to ethical considerations, we unravel the potential and challenges of AI in transforming medical diagnosis. Join us as we explore real-world success stories and peer into the future of healthcare advancements."

Record Your Podcast

With your meticulously crafted script in hand, it's time to breathe life into your podcast using the magic of professional recording equipment. This crucial step is where your voice becomes the conduit for your ideas, stories, and expertise, resonating with your audience and leaving a lasting impression.

As you sit before the microphone, you may find yourself both exhilarated and a tad nervous. But don't worry, because ChatGPT's guidance has fortified your script with compelling content, ensuring that you'll confidently articulate your message. With each word uttered, your passion and enthusiasm will infuse the recording, attracting your listeners and forging a meaningful connection.

To capture your voice with pristine clarity, consider investing in high-quality recording equipment, such as a reliable microphone and a soundproof environment. A professional setup enhances the audio quality, lending a polished and immersive experience to your audience.

The process of recording may take multiple takes, and that's perfectly normal. Embrace the iterative nature of podcasting, allowing yourself the freedom to refine and perfect your delivery. Remember, it's not about achieving perfection in one go but rather about conveying authenticity and sincerity through your voice.

If you want to enhance your podcast's production further, you can approach post-production techniques. Editing software like Adobe Audition or Audacity allows you to fine-tune your recording, removing any unwanted background noise or awkward pauses. It'll provide you with a seamless and professional final product.

Remember, the act of recording your podcast marks a transformative moment, where your ideas materialize into an auditory experience that touches hearts and minds. Embrace the power of your voice, empowered by ChatGPT's creative assistance, and let it take flight in the vast realm of podcasting.

Monetize

Finally, explore monetization options for your podcast. ChatGPT can provide insights on advertising, sponsorships, or setting up premium content for your dedicated listeners. As your podcast gains traction, you can partner with relevant brands or create exclusive content for your loyal audience.

By blending the power of podcasting with ChatGPT's creative assistance, you'll craft a compelling auditory experience that resonates with your audience and unlocks the potential for passive income. Remember, podcasting is a platform that embraces authenticity, so let your passion shine through your voice, and the world will listen. Let's embark on this exciting audio journey together, and watch your podcasting dreams come to life!

Keep These Limitations in Mind While Using ChatGPT for Your Podcast

One important consideration when using ChatGPT for generating passive income is its training data limitation. As a language model, ChatGPT is trained on information up to the year 2021. Any ideas or events that occurred after this date are beyond its knowledge base, and it won't be able to provide specific references to recent developments.

However, despite this limitation, I firmly believe that the benefits of using ChatGPT for income generation far outweigh this drawback. While it may not be up-to-date with the latest events, ChatGPT's capabilities in idea generation, content creation, and problem-solving remain highly valuable and applicable. Its proficiency in aiding with niche research, brainstorming, content generation, and monetization strategies provides a significant advantage in the pursuit of passive income.

Moreover, with the rapid evolution of digital channels and online marketplaces, many fundamental principles and strategies for passive income generation remain relevant over time. The AI's ability to support various income streams, such as blogging, online courses, digital product creation, and more, ensures that its assistance is valuable across a wide range of opportunities.

In my own experience, I have found that the knowledge gap in recent events is a minor trade-off compared to the immense creative assistance and time-saving benefits ChatGPT offers. By staying informed about recent developments independently, users can blend current trends with ChatGPT's creative ideas to create cutting-edge and relevant content.

Ultimately, while ChatGPT might not have access to post-2021 information, its vast potential in guiding users toward passive income success remains unparalleled. As long as users keep themselves updated with the latest trends and combine that knowledge with ChatGPT's creative prowess, they can forge a powerful path toward financial autonomy and capitalize on the numerous opportunities available in the digital landscape.

With ChatGPT's creative power at your disposal, you have discovered the path to compelling content creation, audience engagement, and passive income generation in the world of podcasting. Embrace this authentic platform to showcase your expertise and creativity, while ChatGPT serves as your creative ally, making the process seamless and enjoyable.

As you refine your message and let your voice shine with ChatGPT's assistance, explore monetization opportunities to solidify your presence and share your passion with the world. Dedication and authenticity, combined with ChatGPT's AI-driven guidance, will bring your podcasting dreams within reach.

So, take a deep breath, press that record button, and let your voice soar to new heights of success and fulfillment through the power of soundwave monologues.

PROFIT FROM PERSPECTIVE

UNLEASHING AFFILIATE REVIEW SITES WITH CHATGPT

 "Don't watch the clock; do what it does. Keep going."

SAM LEVENSON

People earn millions by posting articles on things they don't even use. And users often check online reviews before deciding to use a business for the first time. Even online review has a huge impact on their choices, as 82% of consumers trust them and rely on them. The more striking is the fact that 76% of consumers place as much trust in these online reviews as they would in a personal recommendation. This underscores the significance of leveraging the potential of affiliate review sites, empowered by ChatGPT, to provide authentic insights and recommendations that resonate with your audience and drive passive income. With ChatGPT's creative assistance, you have the opportunity to earn the trust of your readers and become a valuable resource in their decision-making process.

How? This is what you will know here. ChatGPT can become your creative ally in crafting persuasive and insightful reviews that drive passive income. So here we will see how ChatGPT can enhance your affiliate marketing efforts, allowing you to monetize your unique perspective and expertise.

HOW TO GENERATE MORE BUCKS WITH LESS HASSLE FROM AFFILIATE MARKETING

Affiliate review sites offer a dynamic and rewarding way to combine your passion for a particular niche with the potential to earn passive income. By utilizing ChatGPT's creative assistance, you can create authentic and engaging reviews that resonate with your audience, cultivating trust and establishing yourself as a knowledgeable authority. This approach not only presents a lucrative income stream but also allows you to share valuable insights and recommendations with the world.

Setting up an affiliate review site has become more accessible than ever, and with ChatGPT by your side, the process becomes even smoother. Whether you are an experienced marketer or a newcomer to the world of affiliate marketing, ChatGPT's user-friendly interface and intuitive guidance ensure a seamless implementation of your ideas.

See how you can get things right in your hands with the following steps.

Choose a Niche

To start, identify a niche that aligns with your interests and expertise. With ChatGPT's help, explore potential niches within a broader category.

"What are some potential niches for affiliate review sites in the health and wellness industry?"

ChatGPT Response: *"Fitness Equipment Reviews," "Natural Supplements and Vitamins," "Healthy Cooking Appliances."*

Setup a Website

Setting up a website is the most vital step in establishing your presence as an affiliate marketer. With ChatGPT's guidance, this process becomes more streamlined and effective. It can create an appealing and user-friendly digital platform that can attract your audience like bees to the hive.

As you are about to make a website, think about its appearance, formation, and accessibility. ChatGPT can provide valuable insights on choosing a visually appealing design that aligns with your niche and brand identity. Whether it's a sleek and modern look for a technology-focused affiliate site or a warm and inviting design for a health and wellness niche, ChatGPT can help you find the perfect balance to leave a lasting impression on your visitors.

Additionally, user experience plays a crucial role in driving engagement and encouraging return visits. ChatGPT's expertise can help you in optimizing the website's layout for easy navigation, ensuring that your audience can access information effortlessly. A clear and intuitive menu structure, strategically placed call-to-action buttons, and well-organized content all contribute to a seamless user experience that keeps visitors coming back for more.

Considering the responsive design aspect is another important thing. ChatGPT can guide you in creating a website that adapts smoothly to various devices, such as mobile phones and tablets. In today's era, a website that is mobile-friendly is essential to attract a broader audience and enhance user satisfaction.

Also, ChatGPT can help you understand the significance of page loading speed. Slow-loading pages can deter visitors and negatively impact search engine rankings. By optimizing images, using the cache, and employing efficient coding practices, you can ensure your website loads swiftly and keeps your audience engaged.

Remember, a well-designed and user-friendly website is your virtual storefront, where your audience can connect with your content and recommendations. With ChatGPT as your creative companion, you have the resources to build an attractive and engaging platform that not only captivates your visitors but also drives them to explore further and take action on your affiliate offers. Embrace the power of website setup with ChatGPT's assistance, and embark on a journey to craft a digital space that reflects your expertise and builds a loyal audience.

Research and Create Quality Content

Utilize ChatGPT's extensive knowledge to conduct research for your product reviews. Seek insights and relevant information to craft well-informed and detailed content that resonates with your audience.

"Help me outline the main points for a product review on 'Fitness Equipment Reviews.'"

ChatGPT Response:

Introduction: Introduce the importance of fitness equipment for home workouts.

- *Features: Highlight key features and benefits of different fitness equipment.*
- *Pros and Cons: Evaluate the effectiveness and limitations of each product.*

- *User Testimonials: Share real-life experiences from users.*
- *Recommendation: Provide a well-informed recommendation based on research.*

Optimize the Content for SEO

Optimizing content for SEO is a crucial aspect of any successful online venture, and with ChatGPT's guidance, you can gain a competitive edge in the digital landscape. SEO plays an amazing role in increasing your website's visibility in search engine results, attracting organic traffic, and ultimately boosting your affiliate revenue.

ChatGPT can be your go-to ally in mastering SEO best practices. It can help you identify relevant keywords and phrases that resonate with your target audience. This will be a huge help for you as it'll lead you to create content that aligns with what users are actively searching for. If you can strategically incorporate these keywords into your blog posts, product reviews, or marketing copy, you can enhance your website's ranking on search engine results pages (SERPs) at the top.

Moreover, ChatGPT can guide you in structuring your content effectively. It can assist in crafting engaging meta titles and meta descriptions that entice users to click through to your site. Compelling meta tags can significantly impact your click-through rates (CTR) and contribute to higher organic traffic.

Additionally, ChatGPT can help you with on-page SEO optimization. From formatting headings to organizing content with bullet points and relevant subheadings, ChatGPT's suggestions can enhance the user experience, keeping visitors engaged and encouraging them to explore more of your site.

If you can implement the SEO best practices, you can create a robust and search engine-friendly website that appeals to both users and search engines alike. And you will get Improved rankings, increased visibility, and a higher likelihood of attracting quality traffic to your affiliate offers or products as a result.

In the competitive online landscape, having content that ranks well on search engines is essential for standing out from the crowd and driving more organic traffic to your website. With ChatGPT's guidance, you can gain a deeper understanding of SEO strategies and tactics, and craft content that not only resonates with your audience but also earns the favor of search engines.

As you optimize your content with ChatGPT's assistance, you'll witness a positive impact on your affiliate revenue. Higher visibility and increased organic traffic translate into more opportunities for visitors to engage with your affiliate offers and convert into paying customers. Ultimately, your well-optimized content will lead to a significant boost in affiliate earnings, solidifying your position in the realm of passive income generation.

Monetization

Explore various monetization strategies, including Amazon Associates and partnerships with other online stores. Allow ChatGPT to assist in brainstorming ideas.

"What are some potential affiliate programs for 'Natural Supplements and Vitamins'?"

ChatGPT Response: *"Vitamin Shoppe, iHerb, Swanson Health, Healthspan."*

Promote Your Website

Promotional efforts are vital to attract visitors to your affiliate review site. Let ChatGPT inspire you with creative promotional strategies.

"Suggest some innovative promotional ideas for 'Healthy Cooking Appliances' reviews."

ChatGPT Response: *"Create cooking tutorial videos featuring the appliances,"* *"Collaborate with health and fitness influencers on social media,"* and *"Offer exclusive discounts or coupon codes to your audience."*

By blending the power of ChatGPT with your expertise, you'll create a captivating affiliate review site that empowers your audience, fosters trust and unlocks the potential for lucrative partnerships. Embrace the creative possibilities, and embark on a journey where your perspective becomes a valuable asset, benefiting both you and your dedicated audience. With ChatGPT as your guide, you're well on your way to profit from the perspective of the world of affiliate marketing. Happy affiliate marketing with ChatGPT by your side!

LOYALTY LADDER

CRAFTING A SUBSCRIPTION SERVICE ON GUMROAD WITH CHATGPT

 "The future depends on what you do today."

MAHATMA GANDHI

Do you know that offering online memberships is the fastest and easiest way to earn money online? And it requires delivering value to customers on a regular basis. So, how can you utilize this information? Well, that's what we will do here. In this chapter, you will see how ChatGPT becomes your trusted companion in building a thriving subscription service on Gumroad. Why Gumroad? Well, some creators have been able to earn over $100,000 selling digital products through Gumroad.

The next few pages explore the art of offering exclusive content to your dedicated audience, forging deeper connections, and unlocking the potential for steady passive income.

Creating a subscription service on Gumroad offers a strategic advantage by fostering loyalty and engagement among your audience. By providing premium content, you not only offer added value to your subscribers but also establish yourself as a trusted authority in your niche. With ChatGPT's creative assistance, the idea becomes not only attainable but also a rewarding endeavor that amplifies your brand presence.

Implementing a subscription service on Gumroad is surprisingly straightforward due to its user-friendly platform. With the help of ChatGPT, you can easily navigate the setup process, manage subscriptions, and deliver exclusive content with ease. The combination of Gumroad's simplicity and ChatGPT's creative insights makes this idea easily achievable for aspiring creators and established artists alike.

HOW TO CREATE A PROFITABLE SUBSCRIPTION SERVICE WITHOUT FACING HARD PARTS

Niche Research

Discover the niche that aligns with your passion and expertise. ChatGPT can provide valuable niche ideas and generate creative prompts to inspire your subscription content. By focusing on a niche you are truly passionate about, you'll cultivate a dedicated subscriber base that shares your enthusiasm.

Here's how ChatGPT can provide insights and generate ideas for subscription content.

"What are some niche ideas for a subscription service in the creative writing domain?"

ChatGPT Response: *"Exclusive Short Story Collection," "Monthly Writing Prompts and Exercises," "Behind-the-Scenes Author Interviews."*

Gumroad Account Creation

Setting up your Gumroad account is the crucial first step toward launching your subscription service and monetizing your unique content. With ChatGPT's guidance, this process becomes smooth and effective, enabling you to create an alluring profile that entices potential subscribers and sets the tone for a captivating subscription journey.

Step-by-Step Guide to Gumroad Account Creation:

1. Sign Up and Account Setup

First, visit the Gumroad website. Click on the "Sign Up" button to begin the account creation process. Now, provide your email address (where required), set a secure password, and choose a unique username for your profile. Lastly, confirm your email to activate your account.

. . .

2. Complete Your Profile

Once your account is set up, proceed to complete your profile. Use ChatGPT's creative assistance to craft a compelling and engaging profile that showcases your subscription service's unique value proposition. Include a catchy profile picture and a visually appealing cover image that reflects the essence of your content.

3. Describe Your Subscription Service

In the profile description section, take ChatGPT's help to write captivating and persuasive descriptions of your subscription offerings. Clearly communicate the benefits and exclusive content that subscribers will receive, enticing them to join your community.

4. Set Subscription Pricing and Tiers

Use ChatGPT to determine the most appropriate pricing for your subscription tiers. Consider offering different tiers with varying levels of access to cater to different audience segments. ChatGPT can provide valuable input on pricing strategies that align with the value of your content.

5. Design Eye-Catching Visuals

Engaging visuals are key to grabbing the attention of potential subscribers. With ChatGPT's assistance, create eye-catching graphics and visuals that suit your brand and subscription service theme. High-quality visuals enhance your profile's appeal and make it more enticing for visitors.

6. Personalize Your Gumroad URL

Customize your Gumroad URL to make it more memorable and branded. ChatGPT can help you brainstorm a unique and catchy URL that reflects your subscription service's identity and makes it easier for users to find and share your page.

7. Integrate Payment Processing

Connect your preferred payment method to your Gumroad account, ensuring a seamless and secure payment experience for your subscribers. ChatGPT can provide insights into various payment options and best practices for a smooth transaction process.

By following this step-by-step guide with ChatGPT's support, you'll establish a captivating Gumroad profile that effectively communicates the value of your subscription service. Engaging descriptions and eye-catching visuals will draw potential subscribers in, setting the stage for a rewarding and captivating subscription journey.

Create Quality Content

Creating exclusive and high-quality content is mandatory for a successful subscription period. With high-quality content, your subscribers will always be eager for your videos and will never think of unsubscribing from your channel. This will lead to increased loyalty and satisfaction, encouraging them to remain subscribed and excitedly anticipate each new release.

Here's where ChatGPT becomes an invaluable asset. By utilizing ChatGPT's creative capabilities, you can gain a unique advantage in outlining, developing, and refining your subscription offerings. ChatGPT's insights will help you generate a diverse range of content ideas, ensuring that your subscription remains fresh and captivating for your audience.

For instance, let's consider the prompt for a "Monthly Writing Prompts and Exercises" subscription.

"Help me outline the main topics for a 'Monthly Writing Prompts and Exercises' subscription."

ChatGPT Response:

- *Short Story Prompts: Stimulate your subscribers' creativity with intriguing story starters that spark their imaginations and inspire unique narratives.*
- *Character Development Exercises: Dive deep into the art of character building and provide exercises that challenge your subscribers to breathe life into their literary personas.*
- *World-Building Challenges: Transport your subscribers to new realms by offering world-building prompts that encourage them to craft immersive and captivating fictional universes.*

- *Genre Exploration and Experimentation: Push the boundaries of creativity with prompts that explore various genres, allowing your subscribers to experiment and refine their writing skills in diverse storytelling styles.*

With ChatGPT's assistance, you'll have a rich palette of content ideas at your disposal, ensuring a consistent flow of engaging and valuable material for your subscribers. By providing them with a diverse range of writing prompts and exercises, you nurture their growth as writers, foster a sense of community, and keep them eagerly awaiting each month's installment.

Promote Your Subscription Content

Effective promotion is essential in attracting subscribers to your service. ChatGPT can brainstorm innovative and strategic promotional ideas to expand your subscriber base. From virtual book launch events to enticing limited-time offers, ChatGPT's suggestions will elevate your marketing efforts.

Here's how ChatGPT can brainstorm innovative promotional strategies to attract subscribers to your service.

"Suggest creative ways to promote the 'Exclusive Short Story Collection' subscription."

ChatGPT Response: *"Host a Virtual Book Launch Event," "Collaborate with Book Clubs and Writing Communities," "Offer Limited-Time Free Trials with Engaging Teasers."*

As you ascend the Loyalty Ladder, guided by ChatGPT's expertise, you'll witness the power of building a dedicated subscriber community on Gumroad. Embrace the opportunity to offer exclusive content, nurture authentic connections, and create a space where your creativity flourishes. With each step, your subscription service will thrive, elevating your brand and unlocking the potential for long-term success. As you reach new heights with your loyal audience, remember that the Loyalty Ladder is an ongoing journey of creativity, authenticity, and shared passion. Happy crafting and exploring the boundless possibilities of subscription success with ChatGPT by your side!

CODE CRAFTED EXTENSIONS

WORDPRESS PLUGIN CREATION USING CHATGPT

 "The scariest moment is always just before you start."

STEPHEN KING

This chapter is all about the exciting world of WordPress Plugin Development with the help of ChatGPT's coding skills. Here, you can learn how to create useful and creative plugins that serve specific needs. After reading the whole chapter, you can find out the potential for passive income through the WordPress Ecosystem.

Creating WordPress plugins offers a powerful opportunity to provide tailored solutions to users within specific niches. With ChatGPT's coding capabilities, you can develop custom plugins that address unique needs, enhancing the overall WordPress experience for your target audience. This idea combines your coding skills with ChatGPT's insights to create functional extensions that have a tangible impact, making it an enticing venture for tech-savvy creators.

Implementing this idea is so feasible, especially with ChatGPT's coding support. WordPress boasts a user-friendly development environment with extensive documentation and a large community of developers. With ChatGPT's assistance, you'll navigate the plugin creation process with greater efficiency, turning your innovative ideas into reality.

HOW TO CREATE AND SELL WORDPRESS PLUGINS WITHOUT KNOWING A WORD OF CODING

Niche Research

Identify specific niches or industries that lack adequate solutions or require enhanced functionalities within WordPress. ChatGPT can assist in researching niches with potential demand for plugins.

"What are some niche ideas that could benefit from a custom WordPress plugin?"

ChatGPT Response:

- *"E-commerce: Streamlined Order Tracking,"*
- *"Education: Interactive Quiz Module,"*
- *"Real Estate: Advanced Property Listing Showcase."*

Brainstorm Functionalities

With ChatGPT's creative insights, brainstorm functionalities that your custom plugin can offer to cater to your chosen niche. Consider unique features and user-friendly interfaces to create a compelling value proposition.

"Suggest innovative functionalities for an E-commerce order tracking plugin."

ChatGPT Response:

- *"Real-time shipping updates,"*
- *"Delivery date estimation,"*
- *"Order history analytics."*

Create the Plugin Development Planning

Use ChatGPT to outline the plugin's development process, including the technologies and coding languages to utilize. Define a clear timeline and prioritize features to streamline the development journey.

Here's a step-by-step guide on how to do it:

First, start by using the right prompt and take help from its response. For example,

"Assist me in outlining the development process for my plugin, specifying the technologies and coding languages to utilize."

ChatGPT Response: To begin, you can prompt ChatGPT with questions like,

- *"What are some recommended technologies for developing a WordPress plugin?"*
- *"Which coding languages are suitable for back-end functionalities in my plugin?"*
- *"What front-end technologies can enhance the user interface of my plugin?"*

Utilize ChatGPT's Expertise: Based on your prompt, ChatGPT will provide valuable insights and recommendations for technologies and coding languages that align with your plugin's objectives and target audience. It can suggest popular front-end frameworks like React or Vue.js for a dynamic user interface or recommend PHP or Python for server-side functionality.

Define a Clear Timeline: ChatGPT can help you set milestones and deadlines for each stage of the development process. You can ask,

- *"How should I structure the timeline for developing my plugin?"*
- *"What are the key milestones I should aim for during the development journey?"*

Prioritize Features: Prompt ChatGPT to prioritize the essential features of your plugin based on their impact on user experience and overall functionality. For example,

"What are the must-have features that I should prioritize in the initial version of the plugin?"

By leveraging ChatGPT's creative assistance, you can create a comprehensive outline for your plugin's development process, incorporating the right technologies, coding languages, and a clear timeline. This collaboration with ChatGPT streamlines your development journey, ensuring you stay organized, make informed decisions, and deliver a high-quality plugin that meets the needs and expectations of your users.

Develop the Plugin

Leverage ChatGPT's coding assistance as you craft the plugin. Utilize WordPress development best practices and integrate functionalities that align with your original vision.

"How do I start coding the Real Estate property listing showcase plugin?"

ChatGPT Response:

- *"Begin by creating custom post types for properties,"*
- *"Design a dynamic search and filtering system,"*
- *"Implement a Google Maps integration for location display."*

Test Your Plugin

Make sure that your plugin functions seamlessly and is compatible with various WordPress versions. Use ChatGPT to create test scenarios and address potential bugs for a polished end product.

To test plugins using ChatGPT, follow these steps:

Define Test Scenarios: Clearly outline the different scenarios you want to assess, covering user interactions, input validations, error handling, and performance testing.

For example,

"Assist me in defining test scenarios for my WordPress plugin."

ChatGPT Response:

- *"Test scenario 1: Validate user registration form fields."*
- *"Test scenario 2: Verify the functionality of the shopping cart in an e-commerce plugin."*
- *"Test scenario 3: Evaluate the loading speed of the plugin on different devices."*

Prepare Test Data: Generate relevant data to simulate various user inputs and edge cases, ensuring comprehensive testing coverage.

For example,

"How do I prepare relevant test data for my plugin?"

ChatGPT Response:

- *"Ensure you have a mix of valid and invalid inputs for testing form fields."*
- *"Create sample product data with different attributes for the e-commerce plugin."*
- *"Generate test data for various screen sizes and devices to assess responsiveness."*

Execute Test Cases: Manually interact with the plugin as users would, observing its behavior under different conditions and analyzing the results.

For example,

"Assist me in executing test cases for my plugin."

ChatGPT Response: "Interact with the registration form using both correct and incorrect data."

- *"Add products to the cart and check if the prices and quantities are accurate."*
- *"Test the plugin on different devices, browsers, and operating systems."*
- *Automate Testing (Optional): Consider automating repetitive test scenarios using testing frameworks and tools for efficiency and consistency.*

For example,

"How can I automate some of the test scenarios for efficiency?"

ChatGPT Response:

- *"Consider using testing frameworks like Selenium or Cypress for automated browser testing."*
- *"Explore API testing tools such as Postman for automated backend testing."*
- *"Utilize test data generation libraries to automate data setup for repetitive tests."*

Analyze Results: Evaluate test outcomes to identify bugs, issues, and areas for improvement, paying attention to error messages, responsiveness, and user feedback.

For example,

"Help me analyze the test results for my plugin."

ChatGPT Response:

- *"Look for any validation errors and ensure error messages are clear and informative."*
- *"Measure the plugin's loading times on different devices to identify performance bottlenecks."*
- *"Collect user feedback and consider their suggestions for further improvements."*

By incorporating ChatGPT's guidance, you can thoroughly test your plugins, identify and resolve issues, and ensure they deliver a seamless and reliable user experience.

Upload Your Plugin

Through ChatGPT's guidance, navigate the process of uploading your plugin to the WordPress repository. Optimize the plugin description and visuals to attract users and encourage downloads.

"What should be included in the plugin description for the E-commerce order tracking plugin?"

ChatGPT Response:

- *"Clearly state real-time tracking capabilities,"*
- *"Highlight supported shipping carriers,"*
- *"Mention compatibility with popular E-commerce platforms."*

Promotion Brainstorming

Explore various monetization strategies for your plugin. ChatGPT can brainstorm ideas such as offering a freemium version with premium add-ons, providing subscriptions for ongoing support, or setting a one-time purchase price.

"How can I promote the Real Estate property listing showcase plugin?"

ChatGPT Response:

- *"Collaborate with real estate agents for endorsements,"*
- *"Offer a limited-time free trial,"*
- *"Create demo videos showcasing plugin features."*

Creating plug-ins doesn't seem much of a hassle now, does it? In this chapter, we've explored code-crafted extensions—WordPress plugin creation with ChatGPT. You've learned to develop custom plugins for specific niches, enhance WordPress functionality, and potentially generate passive income. ChatGPT guided you in brainstorming, planning, coding, and promoting your plugins.

BANKING ON BROWSER BOOSTERS

CREATE A PAID GOOGLE CHROME EXTENSION WITH CHATGPT

 "The only person you are destined to become is the person you decide to be."

RALPH WALDO EMERSON

You don't have to know a single code to earn thousands from plugins and extensions. Nowadays, Chrome extensions offer a swift and efficient means to execute tasks. And users are also willing to pay for high-quality extensions that enhance their browsing experience. So, why not seize this opportunity to tap into a massive user base and generate a steady stream of passive income? If you're worried about complex coding or hefty developer fees, fear not! With the power of ChatGPT, building your own customized Chrome extension is easier than you might think. Let's explore the fascinating world of crafting a paid Google Chrome extension and dive into the effortless implementation process.

A paid Google Chrome extension presents an incredible chance to monetize your skills and ideas. With a vast user base and increasing reliance on extensions, the demand for feature-rich tools is booming. Users are eager to invest in extensions that offer genuine value, whether it's boosting productivity, providing entertainment, or addressing specific needs. By creating a paid extension, you not only tap into this thriving market but also gain financial autonomy and the potential for substantial passive income.

You might think developing a Chrome extension is a daunting task, but with the help of ChatGPT, the process becomes very simple. The AI-powered prompts can generate code snippets, brainstorm features, and guide you through every step of the development journey. Even if you don't have advanced coding skills, ChatGPT empowers you to create a polished and professional extension that stands out in the marketplace.

GUIDE TO CREATING CHROME EXTENSIONS THAT'LL GET YOU EASY CASH

Niche Research

To create a successful Chrome extension, identify a niche or problem it can address. Use ChatGPT to brainstorm niche ideas and narrow down options. Be specific to cater to a well-defined audience.

For example,

"Generate niche ideas for a productivity-focused Chrome extension."

Helpful Response:

- *Task Organizer: Efficiently manage and prioritize tasks.*
- *Focus Timer: Incorporate the Pomodoro technique for enhanced productivity.*
- *Password Manager: Securely store and manage passwords.*
- *Language Translator: Translate web pages into different languages.*
- *Reading Progress Tracker: Track reading progress on web articles."*

Research the market to find gaps and user needs.

For instance,

"Explore the market for task management extensions and identify gaps."

Helpful Response:

- *"High demand for task management, but few offer time tracking. Also, the potential for advanced security password manager."*

With ChatGPT's assistance, refine your niche and create a value-driven Chrome extension that stands out in the market.

Define the Requirements

To create a successful Google Chrome extension, outline clear and concise requirements that shape its functionality and features. Whether it's streamlining tasks, improving user experience, or providing valuable data, these requirements will be the foundation of your extension's essence.

Sample ChatGPT prompt and helpful response,

Prompt:

"You are an AI-powered extension developer tasked with creating a Chrome extension that helps users manage their daily to-do lists. Define the key requirements for the extension, prioritizing user experience and productivity."

Response:

- *"Intuitive interface for easy task management*
- *Add, edit, and delete tasks with due dates*
- *Timely reminders for upcoming tasks*
- *Task categorization and priority settings for efficient workload management."*

With ChatGPT's assistance, craft precise and effective requirements that ensure your Chrome extension becomes a valuable tool for users, meeting their specific needs and enhancing their productivity.

Write the Code

With the AI assistance of ChatGPT, coding for your Chrome extension becomes a piece of cake. No need to be intimidated by complex tasks; ChatGPT can generate code snippets tailored to your specific requirements.

For instance, you can prompt ChatGPT to generate a code snippet for saving user preferences.

"ChatGPT, I need a code snippet to allow users to save preferences in my Chrome extension."

By letting ChatGPT handle repetitive tasks, you can focus on refining your extension's unique features, like building a dropdown menu.

ChatGPT Prompt:

"ChatGPT, can you help me with the code for a dropdown menu in my Chrome extension?"

To these prompts, ChatGPT will literally give you the exact, functioning codes that you need. The best thing is, ChatGPT will take less than a minute to generate these codes.

With ChatGPT's assistance, you can build polished Chrome extensions, saving time and effort while delivering exceptional functionalities to your users. Embrace the power of AI and create extraordinary Chrome extensions effortlessly.

Generate the Plugin

When your development is complete, package your extension for distribution. The process becomes seamless with ChatGPT's guidance. Ensure your extension complies with Google guidelines, and you're on your way to making it accessible to users.

Follow these steps.

- Prepare Required Files: Gather Manifest.json, Popup.html, Popup.js, and Content.js files, vital for the extension's functionality.
- Configure Manifest.json: Set metadata like name, version, description, icons, and permissions.
- Define Default Popup: Specify Popup.html as the default popup file.
- Design User Interface: Customize Popup.html for an appealing layout and user-friendly experience.
- Add JavaScript Interactivity: In Popup.js, handle button clicks and content script interactions.
- Implement Content Script Functionality: Content.js interacts with the web page's content and extracts data.
- Thorough Testing: Test the extension across Chrome versions and devices.
- Comply with Google Guidelines: Ensure adherence to Google's policies for approval.

Test

Once your Chrome extension is developed, thorough testing is vital before releasing it to the public. This step ensures that your extension functions flawlessly and provides a seamless user experience.

Here's what you need to do.

Functionality Testing: Verify that all features and functionalities work as intended. Test each button, option, or action to ensure they deliver the expected results. Address any bugs or glitches that may arise during testing.

Performance Testing: Assess your extension's performance and responsiveness. Check for loading times, memory usage, and overall speed. A well-optimized extension enhances user satisfaction and minimizes potential issues.

Compatibility Testing: Ensure your extension works across various devices and screen sizes. Test it on different operating systems and Chrome versions to guarantee compatibility with a broad user base.

User Feedback: Embrace feedback from real users during the testing phase. Gather insights and suggestions to identify areas for improvement. This user-driven approach will help you refine your extension to meet users' needs.

By conducting comprehensive testing and addressing any identified issues, you can successfully launch a robust and reliable Chrome extension. And, no doubt, it will delight users and foster positive reviews. Remember, continuous improvement based on user feedback is essential for maintaining a successful extension in the long run.

Monetize

You can monetize your Google Chrome extension effectively with a Freemium model, enticing users with a basic version for free and offering premium features in a paid version. Implement a subscription plan for continuous updates and support, giving users the option to subscribe on a monthly or annual basis.

Integrate in-extension purchases to provide users with the opportunity to buy virtual goods or exclusive content directly within your extension. Collaborate with other developers or businesses for cross-promotion, expanding your user base and increasing exposure.

With the help of affiliate marketing to promote relevant products and earn commissions for successful referrals made through your extension. Additionally, offer premium support and personalized services to paid users, delivering value and encouraging customer loyalty. These strategies will help you maximize your extension's value while generating a steady stream of revenue.

Creating a paid Google Chrome extension is a fantastic avenue for generating passive income while offering users valuable solutions. With ChatGPT's assistance, building an extension becomes a straightforward process, even for those without extensive coding knowledge. So, why wait? Dive into this thriving market, unleash your creativity, and embark on a journey of financial autonomy and technological innovation. As an expert in your domain, you have the power to craft extensions that leave a lasting impact on users and open doors to newfound success. Get started today and witness the boundless possibilities of a well-crafted paid Google Chrome extension!

SOME FINAL WORDS

 "Opportunities don't happen. You create them."

CHRIS GROSSER

It is done. This comprehensive guide has taken you on a transformative journey. It explored the myriad possibilities of generating passive income through various digital channels with the aid of ChatGPT. We have navigated through diverse avenues, each offering unique opportunities to create a sustainable source of income.

Starting with the creation of a profitable blog, we have shown you the content creation process, where ChatGPT assists bloggers in generating engaging and SEO-optimized content effortlessly. Moving forward, we've analyzed the online courses and discovered how ChatGPT can transform expertise into a lucrative venture.

Next, we set our sights on the virtual artisan marketplace of Etsy, where ChatGPT proves to be an indispensable tool in crafting and selling digital products that cater to niche audiences. We then explored the realm of ebooks and self-publishing, discovering how ChatGPT can empower indie authors to write captivating books, offering them creative freedom and higher royalties.

Diving towards the video content procedure, we've found the concept of faceless YouTube channels, where ChatGPT's scripting abilities enable the creation of compelling videos without showing one's face. We then ventured into the immersive world of podcasting, where ChatGPT became an ally in generating engaging content and monetization strategies.

The exploration continued with the establishment of affiliate review sites, showcasing ChatGPT's capabilities in providing authentic and persuasive product reviews to influence consumer decisions. We then unlocked the potential of subscription services on Gumroad, highlighting how ChatGPT can help create exclusive content to build audience loyalty.

Finally, we demystified coding and WordPress plugin creation, showcasing how ChatGPT aids in crafting functional and innovative plugins without the need for extensive coding knowledge. We also explored the lucrative opportunity of paid Google Chrome extensions, where ChatGPT helps develop polished extensions catering to niche markets.

Throughout this journey, one key takeaway resonates: With the knowledge obtained in this book, you possess the power to use ChatGPT immediately and start generating passive income. Utilize this moment and take action now, for the possibilities are boundless.

We want you to share your experience by leaving a review of this book on Amazon. Your valuable feedback will help others discover the transformative potential of generating passive income with ChatGPT. Together, let's build a community of empowered individuals, leveraging the power of AI to achieve financial autonomy and create the life they desire.

The path to financial freedom awaits you. Step into the future with ChatGPT as your guide. Start your journey today and unleash your passive income potential with ChatGPT by your side.

REFERENCES

Acast. "How Can Podcasters Use ChatGPT and Other AI Tools to Increase Productivity?" Acast, 2023. https://www.acast.com/blog/podcaster-resources/how-can-podcasters-use-chatgpt-and-other-ai-tools-to-increase-productivity.

BrightLocal. "Local Consumer Review Survey." BrightLocal, 2023, https://www.brightlocal.com/research/local-consumer-review-survey/.

Budd, Colin. 2023. "Building Your First Chrome / Edge Extension with ChatGPT — Zero Programming Required." Medium, March 7, 2023. https://colinbudd.medium.com/building-your-first-chrome-extension-with-chatgpt-zero-programming-required-c646eb0635f7.

Castos. "ChatGPT Prompts." Castos, 2023. https://castos.com/chatgpt-prompts/.

Glassdoor. "Salaries: Blogger." https://www.glassdoor.com/Salaries/blogger-salary-SRCH_KO0,7.htm. Accessed 29 July 2023.

Gumroad. "How to Sell Online Memberships: All You Need to Know." Gumroad Blog, August 3, 2023. https://gumroad.com/blog/how-to-sell-online-memberships-all-you-need-to-know.

Hostinger. "ChatGPT for Blogging." Hostinger, 29 July 2022, https://www.hostinger.com/tutorials/chatgpt-for-blogging#6_Generate_Full_Content.

InVideo For Content Creators. 2023. "How to Create a Faceless YouTube Channel Using AI (ChatGPT & InVideo)." https://www.youtube.com/watch?v=e5ZK8GVtbvQ.

Jennifer Marie. 2023. "How to Use ChatGPT to Create and SELL Digital Printables on Etsy (COMPLETE Guide)." https://www.youtube.com/watch?v=ELokEILd7gU.

Karkovack, Eric. 2023. "So, I Built a WordPress Plugin With ChatGPT - The WP Minute." The WP Minute. March 13, 2023. https://thewpminute.com/so-i-built-a-wordpress-plugin-with-chatgpt/.

Malekos, Nick, and Nick Malekos. 2023. "A.I. Course Creation: How to Use ChatGPT to Create ELearning Content." LearnWorlds, May. https://www.learnworlds.com/chatgpt-create-online-courses/#brainstorm.

Nerdynav. 2023. "How To Create An Online Course With ChatGPT? Definitive Guide." Nerdy Nav (blog). May 23, 2023. https://nerdynav.com/online-course-with-chatgpt/.

Patryk Marketer. 2023. "How To Sell AI Art On Etsy A To Z Blueprint 2023 [FREE Course]." https://www.youtube.com/watch?v=YjNmy96jUmo.

Riverside.fm. "How Much Do Podcasters Make?" Riverside.fm, 2023. https://riverside.fm/blog/how-much-do-podcasters-make.

Tagliaferro, Luca. 2023. "How to Create an SEO Chrome Extension Using ChatGPT." Search Engine Land, June 2, 2023. https://searchengineland.com/chatgpt-seo-chrome-extension-427841.

Trovato, Stephanie. "How To Make Money on Gumroad: Beginner's Guide (2023)." Thinkific. April 30, 2023. https://www.thinkific.com/blog/make-money-on-gumroad/

Tsukayama, Hayley. "Amazon Now Sells More eBooks Than Print Books." The Washington Post, 19 May 2011, www.washingtonpost.com/blogs/faster-forward/post/amazon-now-sells-more-ebooks-than-print-books/2011/05/19/AFTGQH7G_blog.html.

Wisdom Speaks. 2023. "How I Made A Faceless YouTube Channel With ChatGPT (INSANE RESULTS)." https://www.youtube.com/watch?v=OCpShu1h2mQ.

WordsRated. (2023, February 15). Amazon Print Book Sales Statistics. Retrieved from https://wordsrated.com/amazon-print-book-sales-statistics/

THANK YOU

First off, thank you so much for purchasing my book among so many options out there. And thank you for getting this book and for making it all the way to the end.

Before you go, I wanted to ask you for one small favor. **Could you please consider posting a review on the platform? Posting a review is the best and easiest way to support the work of independent authors like me.**

Your feedback will help me to keep writing the kind of books that will help you get the results you want. It would mean a lot to me to hear from you.

Cheers,

Drake Cox

P.S. Just a friendly reminder, here's the link again in case you missed out on the previously mentioned 2 free gifts: **ChatGPT Prompt Library** and **Passive Income Blueprint Checklist.**

You can download it here: https://drakecox.com/bonus

Or, scan the QR code below with your phone.

Manufactured by Amazon.ca
Acheson, AB

15200334R00079